Education for Human Rights

JAGDISH CHAND
Former Deputy Director of Education and
Executive Director of the Delhi Bureau of Textbooks,
Delhi Administration

ANSHAH
Anshah Publishing House

(First Published in 2010)

Rs. 750

ISBN: 978-81-8364-017-6

2014 Impression
(2009, 2007)

Education for Human Rights

Published by:

ANSHAH PUBLISHING HOUSE
LG 18-19, Pankaj Central Market,
Patparganj, Delhi 110092, Ph.: 22235152, 22236152
Email: info@shiprapublication.com
Website: www.shiprapublication.com

Contents

Preface

The theme of the book acquires a special significance in the present day context and has been made part of curriculum for students of education in number of universities. The three themes — Values, Environment and Human Rights, were published in a combined volume in 2005 by Shipra Publications, but keeping in view demand and requirements of the market and students, publishers approached us to bring out each theme separately also and the proposal gladly accepted. I hope users will take its advantage.

Author has made use of various reports, publications, document — primary and secondary sources to make this book students' friendly and express thanks to their authors and publishers. Utmost care has been taken while compiling this book, and regret if there is any omission. It is suggested that students/teachers must consult reference books or encyclopedias to study the subject in deep.

Jagdish Chand

1

Human Rights: Concept, Universal Declaration of Human Rights

ESSENCE OF HUMAN RIGHTS

All Human Beings are Born Free and Equal in Dignity and Rights

Human rights embody the fundamental values of human civilisations.

People are different, and so are their cultures. People live in different ways, and civilisations also differ.

People speak in a variety of languages.

People are guided by different religions.

People are born different colours, and many traditions influence their lives with varying colours and shades.

People dress differently and adapt to their environment in different ways.

People express themselves differently. Music, literature and art reflect different styles as well. *But despite these differences, all people have one single common attribute; they are all human beings – nothing more, nothing less.*

And however different they may be, all cultures embrace certain common principles:

No culture tolerates the exploitation of human beings.

No religion allows the killing of the innocent.

No civilisation accepts violence or terror.

Torture is appalling to the human conscience.

Brutality and cruelty are appalling in every tradition.

In short, these common principles, which are shared by all civilisations, reflect our fundamental human rights. These rights are treasured and cherished by everyone, everywhere.

So cultural relativity should never be used as a pretext to violate human rights, since these rights embody the most fundamental values of human civilisations. The Universal Declaration of Human Rights is needed universally, applicable to both East and West. It is compatible with every faith and religion. Falling to respect our human rights only undermines our humanity.

Let us not destroy this fundamental truth; if we do, the weak will have nowhere to turn. *Shirin Ebadi 2003 Nobel Peace Prize Winner*

CONCEPT AND FOUNDATION OF HUMAN RIGHTS

All human beings are born free and equal in dignity and rights Human rights, as commonly understood, are the rights that every human being is entitled to enjoy freely irrespective of his religion, race, caste, sex and nationality, etc. Because of being a human being, some rights are inherent. Besides, human rights are those rights that pertain to legal rights. A UNESCO publication Human Rights (1996) explains the term 'human rights' as, "Human beings are born equal in dignity and rights. These are moral claims which are inherent in all human individuals by virtue of their humanity alone. These claims are formulated in what we today call human rights. These have been translated into legal rights, established according to the new creating processes of societies, both national and international." It may be stressed that the values of 'dignity' and 'equality' of all human beings which we call human rights are found almost in every religion and philosophical tradition.

HISTORICAL BACKGROUND OF HUMAN RIGHTS

Brief History and Milestones in Human Rights

1. The Magna Carta of A.D. 1215 is considered as the foundation of their liberties by Englishmen. It guaranteed the citizens the freedom from arbitrary imprisonment or from dispossession of property.

All human beings are born free and equal in dignity and rights.

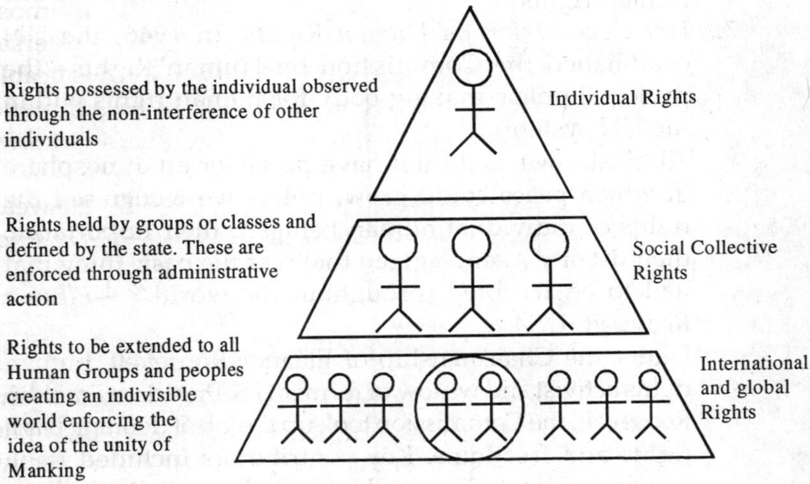

Fig. 1.1: A Holistic View of Human Rights

2. The Bill of Rights (1689), in England, conferred some important rights on the British Parliament. It also declared many actions of King James II illegal.
3. The American Declaration of Independence (July 4, 1776) declared, "We hold these rights to be self-evident, that all men are created equal, that they are endowed by their creator with certain unalienable rights, that among these are life, liberty and the pursuit of happiness."
4. *The Frencg Revolution* (1789) proclaimed the slogans of 'liberty, equality and fraternity.'
5. The League of Nations, set up in 1920 after the First World War, was entrusted with the protection of rights of minorities but it failed in its basic aim of preventing war (Second World War).
6. *The Second World War* (1939–45), proved to be the most destructive war in history. The desire of the nations to make the world free from future wars and ushering in an era of international peace led to the establishment of the UNO (United Nations Organisation) in 1945. Its

Charter contained a number of Articles relating to human rights.

7. *UN Commission on Human Rights*. In 1946, the UN established the Commission on Human Rights—the principal policy-making body for human rights within the UN system.

"Basically we could not have peace, or an atmosphere in which peace could grow, unless we recognised the rights of individual human beings... their importance, their dignity ... and agreed that was the basic thing that had to be accepted throughout the world." —*Eleanor Roosevelt, USA*

Under the Chairmanship of Eleanor Roosevelt, human rights activist and widow of former U.S. President Franklin Roosevelt, the Commission took up the job of defining basic rights and freedoms. Key contributors included Rene Cassin (France), Charles Malik (Lebanon), Peng Chun Chang (China), Hernan Santa Cruz (Chile), Alexandre Bogomolov and Alexei Pavlov (Soviet Union), Lord Dukeston and Geoffrey Wilson (United Kingdom), William Hodgson (Australia) and John Humphrey (Canada).

Originally composed of 18 Member States, the Human Rights Commission now has 53 members who meet annually in Geneva to review human rights issues, develop and codify new international norms, and make recommendations to Governments. Non-governmental organisations play an active role.

8. The General Assembly of the UN passed the Universal Declaration of Human Rights on December 10, 1948.

IMMEDIATE CIRCUMSTANCES LEADING TO THE DECLARATION OF HUMAN RIGHTS

For a long time, several eminent poets, philosophers, politicians, statesmen and thinkers had been pleading for giving due recognition to the dignity and equality of human beings. Fascism of Mussolini of *Italy* and Nazism of Hitler of Germany had shown utter disregard for the human rights. Hitler was guilty of the most inhuman atrocities, especially against the Jews. In the communist regime of the USSR too, individual freedom was given scant regard. The Second World War provided an opportunity. It was realised that massive violations of human rights within the country lead to breach of international peace. The horrors of war confirmed the belief that recognition of the inherent dignity and of equal and inalienable rights of the members of the humankind is the foundation of freedom, justice and peace in the world.

Even during the Second World War, Franklin D. Roosevelt, President of the USA declared in 1941, that the "Four Freedoms" (Freedom of Speech, Freedom of Worship, Freedom of Want and Freedom from Fear) everywhere in the world were the necessary guarantee for peace. The UN Charter reaffirmed its faith in "Fundamental Human Rights is the dignity and worth of the human person."

Thus the stage for the Declaration of Human Rights had already been prepared.

Origin of the Term Human Rights and the Declaration of Human Rights (December 10, 1948)

Ms. Eleanor Roosevelt, Chairperson of the Human Rights Commission set up in 1947, had earlier suggested the term 'human rights.' On the recommendation of the report, the UN declared the Universal Declaration of Human Rights. The declaration contains the Preamble and 30 Articles.

Magna Carta for All Humanity

The Universal Declaration is built on the fundamental principle that human rights are based on the "inherent dignity" of every person. This dignity, and the rights to freedom and equality which derive therefrom, are undeniable.

Although the Declaration does not have the binding force of a treaty, it has acquired universal acceptability. Many countries have cited the Declaration or included its provisions in their basic laws or constitutions. And many human rights covenants, conventions and treaties concluded since 1948 have been built on its principles.

EXTRACTS FROM BILL OF RIGHTS (1689), DECLARATION OF INDEPENDENCE (1776) AND DECLARATION OF THE RIGHTS OF MAN AND OF THE CITIZEN (1789)

1. The Bill of Rights, 1689 (UK)

... the... Lords Spiritual and Temporal and Commons pursuant to their respective letters and elections, being now assembled in a full and free representative of this nation,... do... for the vindicating and asserting their ancient rights and liberties, declare:

- That the pretended power of suspending of laws or the execution of laws by legal authority without consent of Parliament is illegal.
- That the pretended power of dispensing with laws or the execution of laws by legal authority, as it has been assumed and exercised of late, is illegal...
- That levying money for or to the use of the crown by pretence of prerogative without grant of Parliament for longer time or in other manner than the same is or shall be granted is illegal.
- That it is the right of the subjects to petition the king, and all... prosecutions for such petitioning are illegal.
- That the raising or keeping a standing army within the kingdom in time of peace unless it be with consent of Parliament is against law...
- That election of Members of Parliament ought to be free.
- That the freedom of speech and debates or proceedings in Parliament ought not to be impeached or questioned in any court or place out of Parliament.
- That excessive bail ought not to be required, nor excessive fines imposed, nor cruel and unusual punishments inflicted...
- And that for redress of all grievances and for the amending, strengthening, and preserving of the laws, Parliaments ought to be held frequently.
- And they do claim, demand, and insist upon, all the singular, the premises as their undoubted rights and liberties and that no declarations, judgements, doings, or proceedings to the prejudice of the people in any of

the said premises ought in anyway to be drawn here after into consequence or example...

2. The Declaration of Independence, 1776 (USA)

When in the course of human events, it becomes necessary for one people to dissolve the political bands which have connected them with another, and to assume among the Powers of the earth, the separate and equal station to which the Laws of Nature and of Nature's God entitle them, a decent respect to the opinions of mankind requires that they should declare the causes which impel them to the separation.

We hold these truths to be self-evident, that all men are created equal, that they are endowed by their Creator with certain inalienable Rights, that among these are Life, Liberty and the pursuit of Happiness. That to secure these rights, Governments are instituted among Men, deriving their just powers from the consent of the governed. That whenever any form of Government becomes destructive of these ends, it is the Right of the People to alter or to abolish it, and to institute new Government, laying its foundation on such principles and organising its powers in such form, as to them shall seem most likely to effect their Safety and Happiness. Prudence, indeed, will dictate that Governments long established should not be changed for light and transient causes; and accordingly all experience has shown, that mankind are more disposed to suffer, while evils are sufferable, than to right themselves by abolishing the forms to which they are accustomed. But when a long train of abuses and usurpations, pursuing invariably the same Object evinces a design to reduce them under absolute Despotism, it is their right, it is their duty, to throw off such Government, and to provide new Guards for their future security. Such has been the patient sufferance of these Colonies; and such is now the necessity which constrains them to alter their former Systems of Government...

We, therefore, the Representatives of the United States of America, in General Congress, Assembled, appealing to the Supreme Judge of the world for the rectitude of our intentions, do, in the Name, and by the authority of the good People of these Colonies, solemnly publish and declare, That these United Colonies are, and of Right ought to be Free and Independent States; that they are Absolved from all Allegiance to the British Crown, and that all political connection between them and the State of Great Britain, is and ought to be totally dissolved...

3. The Declaration of the Rights of Man and of the Citizen, 1789 (France)

The representatives of the people of France, formed into a National Assembly, considering that ignorance, neglect, or contempt of human rights, are the sole causes of public misfortunes and corruptions of Government, have resolved to set forth in a solemn declaration, these natural imprescriptible, and inalienable rights: that this declaration being constantly present to the minds of the members of the body social, they may be for ever kept attentive to their rights and their duties; that the acts of the legislative and executive powers of government, being capable of being every moment compared with the end of political institutions, may be more respected; and also, that the future claims of the citizens, being directed by simple and incontestable principles, may always tend to the maintenance of the Constitution, and the general happiness.

For these reasons, the National Assembly doth recognise and declare, in the presence of the Supreme Being, and with the hope of his blessing and favour, the following sacred rights of men and of citizens:

I. Men are born, and always continue, free and equal in respect of their rights...

II. The end of all political associations, is the preservation of the natural and imprescriptible rights of man; and the rights are liberty, property, security, and resistance of oppression.

III. The nation is essentially the source of all sovereignty; nor can any individual, or any body of men, be entitled to any authority which is not expressly derived from it.

IV. Political liberty consists in the power of doing whatever does not injure another. The exercise of the natural rights of every man, has no other limits than those which are necessary to secure to every *other* man the free exercise of the same rights; and these limits are determinable only by the law.

V. The law ought to prohibit only actions hurtful to society. What is not prohibited by the law, should not be hindered; nor should anyone be compelled to that which the law does not require.

VI. The law is an expression of the will of the community. All citizens have a right to concur, either personally, or by their representatives, in its formation. It should be the same for all, whether it protects or punishes; and all being equal in its sight, are equally eligible to all honours, places, and employments, according to their different abilities, without any other distinction than that created by their virtues and talents.

VII. No man should be accused, arrested, or held in confinement, except in cases determined by the law, and according to the forms which it has prescribed....

VIII. Every man being presumed innocent till he has been convicted, whenever his detention becomes indispensable, all rigour to him, more than is necessary to secure his person, ought to be provided against by the law.

IX. No man ought to be molested on account of his opinions, not even on account of his religious opinions, provided his avowal of them does not disturb the public order established by the law.

X. The unrestrained communication of ... opinions being one of the most precious rights of man, every citizen may speak, write, and publish freely, provided he is responsible for the abuse of this liberty, in cases determined by the law.

DRAFTING THE UNIVERSAL DECLARATION OF HUMAN RIGHTS (DECEMBER 10, 1948)

The preparatory work for the Universal Declaration of Human Rights is a remarkable and early example of eth Organisation's capacity to bring about international cooperation and consensus. The text was drafted in two years – between January 1947, when the Commission on Human Rights met to prepare an International Bill of Human Rights, and December 1948, when the General Assembly adopted the Universal Declaration. An eight-member drafting committee prepared the preliminary text of the Universal Declaration. The committee, chaired by Mrs. Eleanor Roosevelt, widow of the former United States President, agreed on the central importance of affirming universal respect for human rights and fundamental freedoms, including the principles of non-discrimination and civil and political rights, as well as social, cultural and economic rights. The Commission then revised the draft declaration, in the light of replies from Member States, before submitting it to the General Assembly.

The General Assembly, in turn, scrutinised the document, with the 58 Member States voting a total of 1,400 times on practically every word and every clause of the text. There were many debates. Some Islamic States objected to the articles on equal marriage rights and on the right to change religious belief, for example, while several Western countries criticised the inclusion of economic, social and cultural rights. On 10 December, 1948, the United Nations General Assembly unanimously adopted the Universal Declaration of Human Rights, with 8 abstentions. Since then, 10 December is celebrated every year worldwide as Human Rights Day. The adoption of the Declaration was immediately hailed as a triumph, uniting very diverse and even conflicting political regimes, religious systems and cultural traditions.

Preamble

Whereas recognition of the inherent dignity and of the equal and inalienable rights of all members of the human family is the foundation of freedom, justice and peace in the world,

Whereas disregard and contempt for human rights have resulted in barbarous acts which have outraged the conscience of mankind, and the advent of a world in which human beings shall enjoy freedom of speech and belief and freedom from fear and want has been proclaimed as the highest aspiration of the common people,

Whereas it is essential, if man is to be compelled to have recourse, as a last resort, to rebellion against tyranny and oppression, that human rights should be protected by the rule of law,

Whereas it is essential to promote the development of friendly relations between nations,

Whereas the peoples of the United Nations have in the Charter reaffirmed their faith in fundamental human rights, in the dignity and worth of the human person and in the equal rights of men and women and have determined to promote social progress and better standards of life in larger freedom,

Whereas Member States have pledged themselves to achieve, in cooperation with the United Nations the promotion of universal respect for and observance of human rights and fundamental freedoms,

Whereas a common understanding of these rights and freedoms is of the greatest importance for the full realisation of this pledge.

Now, therefore.

The General Assembly

Proclaims this Universal Declaration of Human Rights as a common standard of achievement for all peoples and all nations, to the end that every individual and every organ of society, keeping this Declaration constantly in mind, shall strive by teaching and education to promote respect for these rights and freedoms and by progressive measures, national and international, to secure their universal and effective recognition and observance, both among the peoples of Member States themselves and among the peoples of territories under their jurisdiction.

Article 1

All human beings are born free and equal in dignity and rights. They are endowed with reason and conscience and should act towards one another in a spirit of brotherhood.

Article 2

Everyone is entitled to all the rights and freedoms set forth in this Declaration, without distinction of any kind, such as race, colour, sex, language, religion, political or other opinion, national or social origin, property, birth or other status. Furthermore, no distinction shall be made on the basis of the political, jurisdictional or international status of the country or territory to which a person belongs, whether it be independent, trust, non-self-governing or under any other limitation of sovereignty.

Article 3

Everyone has the right to life, liberty and security of person.

Article 4

No one shall be held in slavery or servitude; slavery and the slave trade shall be prohibited in all their forms.

Article 5

No one shall be subjected to torture or to cruel, inhuman or degrading treatment or punishment.

Article 6

Everyone has the right to recognition everywhere as a person before the law.

Article 7

All are equal before the law and are entitled without any discrimination to equal protection of the law. All are entitled to equal protection against any discrimination in violation of this Declaration and against any incitement to such discrimination.

Article 8

Everyone has the right to an effective remedy by the competent national tribunals for acts violating the fundamental rights granted him by the constitution or by law.

Article 9

No one shall be subjected to arbitrary arrest, detention or exile.

Article 10

Everyone is entitled in full equality to a fair and public hearing by an independent and impartial tribunal, in the determination of his rights and obligations and of any criminal charge against him.

Article 11

1. Everyone charged with a penal offence has the right to be presumed innocent until proved guilty according to law in a public trial at which he has had all the guarantees necessary for his defence.
2. No one shall be held guilty of any penal offence on account of any act or omission which did not constitute a penal offence, under national or international law, at the time when it was committed. Nor shall a heavier penalty be imposed than the one that was applicable at the time the penal offence was committed.

Article 12

No one shall be subjected to arbitrary interference with his privacy, family, home or correspondence, nor to attacks upon his honour and reputation. Everyone has the right to the protection of the law against such interference or attacks.

Article 13

1. Everyone has the right to freedom of movement and residence within the borders of each State.
2. Everyone has the right to leave any country, including his own, and to return to his country.

Article 14

1. Everyone has the right to seek and to enjoy in other countries asylum from persecution.

This right may not be invoked in the case of prosecutions genuinely arising from non-political crimes or from acts contrary to the purposes and principles of the United Nations.

Article 15

1. Everyone has the right to a nationality.

2. No one shall be arbitrarily deprived of his nationality nor denied the right to change his nationality.

Article 16

1. Men and women of full age, without any limitation due to race, nationality or religion have the right to marry and to found a family. They are entitled to equal rights as to marriage, during marriage and at its dissolution.
2. Marriage shall be entered into only with and free and full consent of the intending spouses.
3. The family is the natural and fundamental group unit of society and is entitled to protection by society and the State.

Article 17

1. Everyone has the right to own property alone as well as in association with others.
2. No one shall be arbitrarily deprived of his property.

Article 18

Everyone has the right to freedom of thought, conscience and religion; this right includes freedom to change his religion or belief, and freedom, either alone or in community with others and in public or private, to manifest his religion or belief in teaching, practice, worship and observance.

Article 19

Everyone has the right to freedom of opinion and expression; this right includes freedom to hold opinions without interference and to seek, receive and impart information and ideas through any media and regardless of frontiers.

Article 20

1. Everyone has the right to freedom of peaceful assembly and association.
2. No one may be compelled to belong to an association.

Article 21

1. Everyone has the right to take part to public service in his country.

3. The will of the people shall be the basis of the authority of government; this will shall be expressed in periodic and genuine elections which shall be by universal and equal suffrage and shall be held by secret vote or by equivalent free voting procedures.

Article 22

Everyone, as a member of society, has the right to social security and is entitled to realisation, through national effort and international cooperation and in accordance with the organisation and resources of each State, of the economic, social and cultural rights indispensable for his dignity and the free development of his personality.

Article 23

1. Everyone has the right to work, to free choice of employment, to just and favourable conditions of work and to protection against unemployment.
2. Everyone, without any discrimination, has the right to equal pay for equal work.
3. Everyone who works has the right to just and favourable remuneration ensuring for himself and his family and existence worthy of human dignity, and supplemented, if necessary, by other means of social protection.
4. Everyone has the right to form and to join trade unions for the protection of his interests.

Article 24

Everyone has the right to rest and leisure including reasonable limitation of working hours and periodic holidays with pay.

Article 25

1. Everyone has the right to a standard of living adequate for the health and well-being of himself and of his family including food, clothing, housing and medical care and necessary social services, and the right to security in the event of unemployment, sickness, disability, widowhood,

old age or other lack of livelihood in circumstances beyond his control.

2. Motherhood and childhood are entitled to special care and assistance. All children, whether born in or out of wedlock, shall enjoy the same social protection.

Article 26

1. Everyone has the right to education. Education shall be free, at least in the elementary and fundamental stages. Elementary education shall be compulsory. Technical and professional education shall be made generally available and higher education shall be equally accessible to all on the basis of merit.
2. Education shall be directed to the full development of the human personality and to the strengthening of respect for human rights and fundamental freedoms. It shall promote understanding, tolerance and friendship among all nations, racial or religious groups, and shall further the activities of the United Nations for the maintenance of peace.
3. Parents have a prior right to choose the kind of education that shall be given to their children.

Article 27

1. Everyone has the right freely to participate in the cultural life of the community, to enjoy the arts and to share in scientific advancement and its benefits.
2. Everyone has the right to the protection of the moral and material interests resulting from any scientific, literary or artistic production of which he is the author.

Article 28

Everyone is entitled to a social and international order in which the rights and freedoms set forth in this Declaration can be full realised.

Article 29

1. Everyone has duties to the community in which alone the free and full development of his personality is possible.

2. In the exercise of his rights and freedoms, everyone shall be subject only to such limitations as are determined by law solely for the purpose of securing due recognition and respect for the rights and freedoms of others and of meeting the just requirements of morality, public order and the general welfare in a democratic society.
3. These rights and freedoms may in no case be exercised contrary to the purposes and principles of the United Nations.

Article 30

Nothing in this Declaration may be interpreted as implying for any State, group or person any right to engage in any activity or to perform any act aimed at the destruction of any of the rights and freedoms set forth herein.

BROAD CLASSIFICATION OF HUMAN RIGHTS – NO. 1

Broad Classification of Human Rights – No. 1

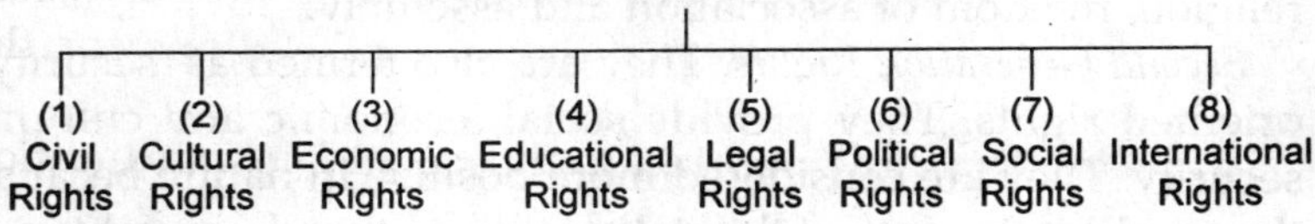

Civil Rights– Articles, 1, 2, 3, 4, 5, 9, 12, 13, 15, 17.
Cultural Rights– Articles 24 and 27.
Economic Rights– Articles 16, 23 and 25.
Educational Rights– Article 26.
Legal Rights– Articles 6, 7, 8, 10, 11.
Political Rights– Articles 18, 19, 20, 21 and 30.
Social Rights– Articles 22 and 29.
Internmational Rights– Articles 14 and 28.

Broad Classification of Human Rights—No. 2

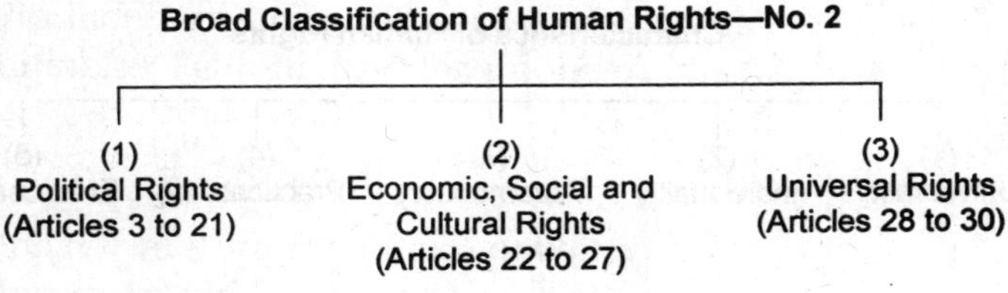

Broad Classification of Human Rights—No. 3

(1) Civil and Political Rights (Articles 3 to 21)

(2) Economic, Social and Cultural Rights (Articles 22 to 27)

(3) Universal Human Rights (Articles 28 to 30)

Broad Classification of Human Rights—No. 4

(1) First Generation Rights

(2) Second Generation Rights

(3) Third Generation Rights

First Generation Rights. These are primarily concerned with civil and political rights of individuals. They include (i) Right to life, liberty, security, freedom from torture and slavery, political participation, right to property, marriage, fundamental freedoms of opinion, expression, thought, conscience and religion, freedom of association and assembly.

Second Generation Rights. They are also termed as 'security' oriented rights. They provide social, economic and cultural security. They are considered more positive in nature because they make it the duty of the state to ensure that these rights are realised.

Third Generation Rights. These rights emerged recently on the basis of international consensus. These include cultural, developmental and environmental rights. Basically, they relate to groups rather than to individuals. They are especially the concern of the developing countries.

It may be remembered that since several human rights overlap and they cannot be divided into watertight compartments.

Characteristics of Human Rights

(1) Universality

(2) Individuality

(3) Paramountcy

(4) Practicability

(5) Enforceability

According to Macfarlane, they are universal in the sense that they are "rights of all people at all times and in all situations." The U.N. Declaration also professes to be a statement of human rights irrespective of the type of social and political order under which people happen to live.

Secondly, the human rights are individualistic because the concept of human right is derived from the acceptance of man as free and equal in dignity and rights. He is endowed with reason and conscience, and capable of moral choice and free activity. Where the worth of individual is not recognised, there is no place of rights.

Thirdly, the human rights are paramount in the sense that 'no one can be deprived of human rights without a grave affront to justice.' Human Rights represent certain freedoms which are sacred and which should never be invaded. The State should not override them at any cost and they can be exercised in spite of the law of the country.

Fourthly, the human rights are practical in the sense that they are the claims which are not physically impossible to be realised. Moreover, they can be extended to the majority and should not be restricted to a small minority. It does not mean that everybody can be made equal, but, nevertheless, he has a claim to an adequate livelihood, basic economic and social needs with minimum basic rights to existence.

Lastly, these rights are enforceable, because, otherwise, their fruits cannot reach the people. National Commission on Human Rights have been set up to ensure their implementation.

SIGNIFICANCE OF HUMAN RIGHTS

1. *Means of Inspiration.* The Declaration serves as a great source of inspiration to the millions of people especially who are oppressed and remained for long under colonial regimes.
2. *Instruments of Maximum Welfare and Happiness of the Individual.* The implementation of the human rights would go a long way to provide a happy, healthy and satisfying life to millions of individuals.

3. *Recognition of Elements of Dignity and Equality.* Keeping in view this factor, states and societies, take several measures towards the fulfilment of this ideal.
4. *Basic for Human Life.* It is recognised that human rights are basic for the optimum development of the individuals. They indicate the basic needs and demands of the individuals which must be fulfilled. Without the fulfilment of these, a human being cannot remain a human being in the true sense.
5. *Inclusion in the Constitutions.* Keeping in view the importance of the human rights, states incorporate these in their constitutions which mirror their hopes, ideals, aspirations and values.

THE UNIVERSAL DECLARATION OF HUMAN RIGHTS AT A GLANCE

This abbreviated version of the 30 Articles of the Universal Declaration of Human Rights provides an overview of the principal rights and freedoms that are every person's birthright.

The first two articles are fundamental principles underlying all human rights. Articles 3 to 21 comprise civil and political rights. Articles 22 to 27 refer to economic, social and cultural rights. The last three articles provide a framework of solidarity safeguarding the universal enjoyment of all human rights.

Article 1	Right to freedom and equality in dignity and rights
Article 2	Freedom from discrimination
Article 3	Right to life, liberty and security of person
Article 4	Right to freedom from slavery and servitude
Article 5	Right to freedom from torture or degrading treatment
Article 6	Right to recognition as a person before the law
Article 7	Right to equal consideration before the law
Article 8	Right to remedy through a competent tribunal
Article 9	Right to freedom from arbitrary arrest or exile
Article 10	Right to a fair trial or public hearing
Article 11	Right to be considered innocent until proven guilty

Article 12	Freedom from interference with privacy, including home, family and correspondence
Article 13	Right to freedom of movement and residence in one's own country and to leave and return at will
Article 14	Right to asylum
Article 15	Right to a nationality and freedom to change it
Article 16	Right to marriage and protection of family
Article 17	Right to own property
Article 18	Freedom of belief and religion
Article 19	Freedom of opinion and information
Article 20	Right to peaceful assembly and association
Article 21	Right to participate in government and in free elections and to equal access to public service
Article 22	Right to social security
Article 23	Right to work and fair pay for work
Article 24	Right to rest and leisure
Article 25	Right to adequate standard of living for health and well-being
Article 26	Right to education
Article 27	Right to participate in the cultural life of the community
Article 28	Right to social order assuring human rights
Article 29	Responsibility to community essential to free and full development of the individual
Article 30	Right for protection of these rights from State or other interference.

BRIEF ANALYSIS AND REVIEW OF DECLARATION OF HUMAN RIGHTS

For the first time in history, the international community embraced a document considered to have universal value — a common standard of achievement for all peoples and all nations. Its Preamble acknowledges the importance of a human rights legal framework for maintaining international peace and security, stating that recognition of the inherent dignity and equal and inalienable rights of all individuals is the foundation of freedom, justice and peace in the world.

Elaborating the United Nations Charter's declared purpose of promoting social progress and well-being in larger freedom, the Declaration gives equal importance to economic, social and cultural rights and to civil rights and political liberties, and affords them the same degree of protection. The Declaration has inspired more than 60 international human rights instruments, which together constitute a comprehensive system of legally binding treaties for the promotion and protection of human rights.

The Universal Declaration covers the range of human rights in 30 clear and concise articles. The first two articles lay down the universal foundation of human rights: human beings are equal because of their shared essence of human dignity; human rights are universal, not because of any State or international organisation, but because they belong to all of humanity. The two articles assure that human rights are the birthright of everyone, not privileges of a select few, nor privileges to be granted or denied. Article 1 declares that "all human beings are born equal in dignity and rights. They are endowed with reason and conscience and should act towards one another in a spirit of brotherhood." Article 2 recognises the universal dignity of a life free from discrimination. "Everyone is entitled to all the rights and freedoms set forth in this Declaration, without distinction of any kind such as race, colour, sex, language, religion, political or other opinion, national or social origin, property, birth or other status."

The first cluster of articles, 3 to 21, sets forth civil and political rights to which everyone is entitled. The right to life, liberty and personal security, recognised in Article 3, sets the base for all following political rights and civil liberties, including freedom from slavery, torture and arbitrary arrest, as well as the rights to a fair trial, free speech and free movement and privacy.

The second cluster of articles, 22 to 27, sets forth the economic, social and cultural rights to which all human beings are entitled. The cornerstone of these rights is Article 22, acknowledging that, as a member of society, everyone has the right to social security and is therefore entitled to the realisation of the economic, social and cultural rights "indispensable" for his or her dignity and free and full personal development. Five articles elaborate the rights necessary for the enjoyment of the fundamental right to social security, including economic rights related to work, fair remuneration and leisure, social rights concerning an adequate standard of living for health, well-being and education, and the right to participate in the cultural life of the community.

The third and final cluster of articles, 28 to 30, provides a larger protective framework in which all human rights are to be universally enjoyed. Article 28 recognises the right to a social and international order that enables the realisation of human rights and fundamental freedoms. Article 29 acknowledges that, along with rights, human beings also have obligations to the community which also enable them to develop their individual potential freely and fully. Article 30, finally, protects the interpretation of the articles of the Declaration from any outside interference contrary to the purposes and principles of the United Nations. It explicitly states that no State, group or person can claim, on the basis of the Declaration, to have the right to engage in any activity or to perform any act aimed at the destruction of any of the rights and freedoms set forth in the Universal Declaration.

UN AND DISSEMINATION OF THE KNOWLEDGE OF THE HUMAN RIGHTS

The General Assembly of the UN has adopted several resolutions for ensuring better knowledge of human rights.

Major types of activities in this regard include:

1. Production and dissemination of printed matter on human rights.
2. Organisation of workshops and seminars on human rights.
3. Granting of fellowship for human rights.
4. Establishment and creation of national human rights institutions.
5. Use of media for the promotion of human rights.

World Conference on Human Rights

The United Nations designated 1968 as the International Year for Human Rights to mark the twentieth anniversary of the Universal Declaration on Human Rights, and convened an International Conference on Human Rights in Tehran, Iran, to enhance national and international human rights efforts and initiatives. After evaluating the impact of the Universal Declaration on national legislation and judicial decisions, the Conference approved the Proclamation of Tehran, which formulated a programme for the future, addressing the problems of colonialism, racial discrimination, illiteracy and the protection of the family. The Tehran Proclamation emphasised particularly the principle of non-discrimination, condemning the policy of apartheid as a "crime against humanity," and urged the international community to ratify the International Covenants on Civil and Political Rights and on Economic, Social and Cultural Rights adopted by the United Nations two years earlier.

The World Conference on Human Rights in Vienna reassessed the progress of United Nations human rights work over the years. The Vienna Conference was marked by an unprecedented degree of support by the international human rights community. Some 7,000 participants, including delegations from 171 States and representatives of more than 840 non-governmental organisations, gathered for two weeks to set out a revitalised programme for global human rights action. There was broad consensus that, with fundamental rights codified and the essential machinery in place, it was time to implement the established human rights standards and norms with greater vigilance.

In adopting the *Vienna Declaration and Programme of Action* by consensus, the World Conference reaffirmed the centrality of the Universal Declaration for human rights protection, and recognised, for the first time unanimously, the right to development as an inalienable right and an integral part of international human rights law. The Conference also emphasised that, as human rights are universal and indivisible as well as interrelated and interdependent, they should be promoted in equal manner. The delegates rejected arguments that some human rights were optional or subordinate to cultural traditions and practices. The Vienna Conference thus gave high priority to preserving the integrity of the Universal Declaration. Giving new impetus to the worldwide implementation of human rights norms, the Conference emphasised that most violations could be addressed by forcefully implementing existing norms through the mechanisms already available.

PROMOTION AND PROTECTION OF HUMAN RIGHTS BY UN

Through the international machinery, the United Nations is at work on several fronts:

As Global Conscience Keeper. The United Nations has set a pace in establishing minimum standards of acceptable behaviour by nations. Human rights declarations and conventions are adopted by the General Assembly, underscoring their universality.

As Lawmaker. An unprecedented codification of international law has taken place. Those human rights pertaining to women, children, prisoners and detainees, and mentally disabled persons, as well as violations such as genocide, racial discrimination and torture, to name just a few, are now a major part of international law.

As Monitor. The United Nations has played a central role in ensuring that human rights are not just defined in the abstract, but also put into practice. The International Covenants on Civil and Political Rights and on Economic, Social and Cultural Rights (1966) are among the earliest examples of treaties that empower international bodies to monitor how states live up to their commitments. Treaty bodies, Special Rapporteurs and Working Groups of the Commission of Human Rights each have procedures and mechanisms to monitor compliance with international standards and investigate allegations of human rights abuses. Their resolutions on specific cases carry a moral weight that few governments are willing to defy.

As Nerve-Centre. The office of the High Commissioner for Human Rights (OHCHR) receives communications from groups and individuals claiming violations of their human rights. OHCHR maintains a 24-hours fax hotline in Geneva to receive emergency complaints about violations of human rights.

As Researcher. The data compiled by the United Nations on human rights issues is indispensable to the development and application of human rights law.

As Forum of Appeal. Under the First Optional Protocol to the International Covenant on Civil and Political Rights, the International Convention on the Elimination of All-Forms of Racial Discrimination and the Convention Against Torture, individual complaints may be brought against states that have accepted the relevant international legal procedures, once all domestic remedies have been exhausted.

As Fact Finder. The Commission on Human Rights has established mechanisms to monitor and report on the incidence of certain kinds of abuses, and on violations in a specific country.

UN ORGANISATIONS FOR PROMOTION OF HUMAN RIGHTS

1. *The United Nations Commission on Human Rights*. A major United Nations body working to promote and protect human rights is the 53-member United Nations Commission on Human Rights, which was established in 1946 by ECOSOC (Economic and Social Council). The Commission provides overall policy guidance, studies human rights problems, develops and codifies new international norms and monitors the observance of human rights around the world.

   The Commission provides a forum for states, intergovernmental organisations and NGOs to voice their concerns about human rights issue. Made up of 53-Member States elected for three-year terms, the Commission meets for six weeks each year in Geneva.
2. *Human Rights Committee*. The International Covenants (1968) established an 18-member Human Rights Committee, which considers reports submitted by states

parties on measures taken to implement the Covenants' provisions. The Committee makes specific recommendations to the states parties, based on its study of their reports. The Committee also makes general comments on the scope and meaning of certain provisions of the Covenant which are designed to help states parties to implement the provisions.

3. *The High Commissioner for Human Rights.* The post of High Commissioner for Human Rights was created in 1993 to strengthen the coordination and impact of United Nations human rights activities. Appointed for a four-year term, the High Commissioner is charged with many tasks, including: promoting international cooperation for human rights; stimulating and coordinating action on human rights in the United Nations system; and assisting in developing new human rights standards and promoting ratification of human rights treaties. The High Commissioner is also mandated to respond to serious violations of human rights and to undertake action to prevent violations.
4. *The Office of the High Commissioner for Human Rights* (OHCHR) is the focal point for United Nations human rights activities and serves as the secretariat for the Commission on Human Rights, the treaty bodies (expert committees monitoring treaty compliance) and other United Nations human rights organs. In addition to the regular budget, some of its activities are financed through voluntary or trust funds.
5. *Centre for Human Rights.* The Centre for Human Rights is located at Geneva in Switzerland. Since 1955, the Centre for Human Rights has administered a programme of advisory services and technical assistance which aims to foster a climate conducive to respect for human rights.

The programme encompasses a wide range of activities from the training of public officials and law enforcement personnel to the translation and dissemination of human rights instruments and information. Governments are provided with expert assistance in a number of crucial areas including election procedure, legislative and constitutional drafting and the development of effective and accessible legal system.

UN COVENANTS AND CONFERENCE ON HUMAN RIGHTS

The Declaration on Human Rights was required to be supported by legal actions. For this purpose, the General Assembly adopted in 1966 two covenants on civil and political rights. (1) International Covenant on Civil and Political Rights (2) International Covenant on Economic, Social Rights. These came into force in 1976. Nearly 150 states including India have ratified these covenants.

UN CONFERENCES ON HUMAN RIGHTS

1968 The International Conference on Human Rights at Tehran – first worldwide conference devoted exclusively to human rights.

1993 The World Conference on Human Rights held at Vienna.

Vienna Declaration

Democracy, development and respect for human rights and fundamental freedoms are interdependent and mutually reinforcing.

The Convention also stressed the rights and protection of the following categories:

(a) Women's rights.
(b) Rights of indigenous people.
(c) Rights of refugees.
(d) Rights of stateless persons.
(e) Rights of children.
(f) Rights of physically and mentally disabled persons.
(g) Protection of detainees.
(h) Protection of the migrant workers.

In accordance with the recommendations of the Vienna Conference, the United Nations Decade for Human Rights Education (1995–2004) was proclaimed. Coordination for the implementation of the Decade's Plan of Action was entrusted to the United Nations High Commissioner for Human Rights.

World Conferences on Rights of Labour and Rights of Women, Right to Development have been held.

UN CONTRIBUTION IN PROMOTING HUMAN RIGHTS

One of the great achievements of the United Nations is the creation of a comprehensive body of human rights law—one to which all nations can subscribe. At the same time, the UN has created effective mechanisms to protect and promote human rights.

- The UN created the first global Bill of Human Rights: the 1948 Universal Declaration of Human Rights, and the two 1966 International Human Rights Covenants (on civil and political rights, and on economic, social and cultural rights), which make many of the Declaration's provisions legally binding on states.
- The UN has helped negotiate more than 80 international treaties fostering political, civil, economic, social and cultural rights.
- The UN has been instrumental in securing universal recognition of crucial rights: for instance, the rights of women and the right of all peoples to development.
- Many peace-keeping operations include provisions for protecting the human rights of the population.
- The UN High Commissioner for Human Rights seeks to prevent violations, investigates abuses in specific countries and engages in dialogue with governments.
- The UN Secretary-General and the High Commissioner confidentially raise human rights concerns with governments on items such as the release of prisoners and the commutation of death sentences.
- By investigating and reporting on complaints of violations, the UN Commission on Human Rights helps

focus world attention, generating international pressure on governments to improve their human rights practices.

- UN human rights experts monitor the human rights situation in a specific country, or widespread violations such as torture, alerting the international community to human rights abuses.
- A 24-hour fax hotline to report violations is in operation at the UN Office in Geneva.
- The UN Centre for Human Rights assists in all the above efforts; it also helps governments to fulfil their human rights responsibilities by providing technical assistance in matters such as the training of police, the drafting of laws and the improvement of legal systems.

HUMAN RIGHTS FOR DIFFERENT SECTIONS

1. End of Apartheid and Racial Discrimination

In 1952, when the General Assembly took up the issue of apartheid in South Africa, the United Nations placed itself at the forefront of international efforts to end this "crime against humanity."

Constant vigilance and pressure over the years resulted in the dismantling of the apartheid system in South Africa in 1994.

The fight against racism continues around the world. The United Nations strives to raise awareness to combat this social injustice. The years 1993–2003 had been proclaimed the Third Decade to Combat Racism and Racial Discrimination.

2. Women's Rights and Human Rights

Respect for human rights will not be universal until women's rights are recognised and protected.

The Convention on the Elimination of All Forms of Discrimination against Women was adopted by the General Assembly in 1979 and has now been ratified by over 160 countries. Compliance is monitored by the Committee on the Elimination of Discrimination against Women (CEDAW).

UNIFEM, the UN Development Fund for Women, has a special programme which works to promote and protect women's rights.

But around the world, cultural and traditional forces continue to subject women to secondary status. Too often violations remain hidden and silent. The global women's movement, a new cultural force, is working to break the silence and demands that rights for women everywhere be respected and upheld.

3. The Rights of Indigenous People

Throughout history, the world's indigenous people – an estimated 300 million in more than 70 countries – have suffered at the hands of colonisers and others seeking territory and riches.

The United Nations Working Group on Indigenous Populations, which has been meeting since 1982, works to promote indigenous people's rights. Members have drafted a Declaration on the Rights of Indigenous Peoples which, if adopted, will represent a major step forward.

The General Assembly's proclamation of 1993 as the International Year of the World's Indigenous People and 1995–2004 as the International Decade of the World's Indigenous People was an effort to strengthen international cooperation for solving the problems faced by indigenous communities.

4. The Rights of the Child

Respect for human rights begins with the way society treats its children.

On 20 November 1989, the UN General Assembly adopted the historic Convention on the Rights of the Child. To date it has been ratified by 191 countries.

This landmark convention is the most complete statement of children's rights ever and is the first to give these rights the force of international law.

5. Human Rights of Migrant Workers

Never before have so many people crossed borders in search of better lives.

And experts predict that the number of migrant workers – estimated at nearly 100 million – will only rise with increased globalisation.

But where they seek improved living standards, many migrant workers find instead discrimination and abuse.

In 1990, following 10 years of negotiations, the General Assembly adopted the International Convention on the Protection of the Rights of All Migrant Workers and Members of Their Families.

However, the treaty has not yet entered into force because it needs ratification by 20 Governments and as of May 1998 had only been ratified by nine: Bosnia and Herzegovina, Cape Verde, Colombia, Egypt, Morocco, Philippines, Seychelles, Sri Lanka and Uganda.

6. Human Rights of Disabled Persons

Often marginalised in society, disabled persons constitute ten per cent of the world's population.

They are frequently denied the most basic educational opportunities. Physical restrictions bar them from public buildings and transport. Social attitudes exclude them from cultural life and normal relationships. Prejudice and ignorance often lead to unnecessary institutionalisation.

In striving for a consensus on the protection of the rights of disabled persons, the General Assembly in 1993 adopted the Standard Rules on the Equalisation of Opportunities for Persons with Disabilities.

The rules offer an instrument for policy-making in the quest for a "society for all" which recognises the development of the human potential of each person.

7. Human Rights, Development and Democracy

Full human dignity means not only freedom from torture, but also freedom from hunger. It means freedom to vote and the right to education. It means freedom of expression and the right to health. It means the right to enjoy all rights without discrimination.

In 1986, the UN General Assembly adopted the Declaration on the Right to Development, which states that:

"The human person is the central subject of development and should be the participant and beneficiary of the right to development."

However, despite international efforts, over one billion people nearly one-sixth of world population today live in absolute poverty on less than $1 a day.

Good governance, democracy and popular participation are increasingly viewed as key agents in the quest for economic and social development, as are equitable trade terms and debt relief.

8. Human Rights and Humanitarian Assistance

Around the world, human rights are an integral part of situations in which humanitarian assistance is required. Victims might be refugees, displaced people or other civilians caught up in internal conflicts. Still, their plight is the same. Their human rights are likely to have been violated and they need protection and assistance.

"Human rights violations are a major cause of refugee flows," says Sadako Ogata, the UN High Commissioner for Refugees. Refugees also suffer a range of abuses once they leave their homes, from piracy and rape to arrest, detention, torture and discrimination in the country to which they have escaped.

The international community is increasingly focusing on preventive action to address problems before they become humanitarian emergencies.

9. Human Rights and International Criminal Court

High hopes have been raised by the June 1998 conference in Rome to establish an international criminal court, which would form a vital part of an emerging system of international human rights protection.

For nearly half a century, the United Nations has recognised the need to establish an international criminal court to prosecute and punish persons responsible for crimes against humanity.

In the absence of such a court, two ad-hoc criminal courts have been set up to judge war crimes in the former Yugoslavia and in Rwanda.

OVERVIEW OF THE IMPACT OF THE UNIVERSAL DECLARATION OF HUMAN RIGHTS

Leah Levin, in a UNESCO publication entitled *"Human*

Rights: Questions and Answers" has explained the impact of the Declaration as under: "Although the Universal Declaration of Human Rights is not legally binding, over the years its main principles have acquired the status of standards which should be respected by all States. When the Declaration was adopted, there were only fifty-eight Member States of the United Nations. Since that time, this number has more than tripled. The continuing impact of the Declaration and the use made of it bears out its universal acceptance, and it has become a common reference in human rights for all nations.

The Universal Declaration, together with the Charter, served both as an inspiration and a means for the millions of people under colonial rule to achieve self-determination in the 1950s and 1960s, and many incorporated the provisions of the Declaration in their constitutions.

The consensus of the international community was reflected at the International Conference on Human Rights in Tehran in 1968—that the Universal Declaration 'states a common understanding of the people of the world concerning the inalienable and inviolable rights of all members of the human family and constitutes an obligation for the members of the international community.' Twenty-five years later, at the World Conference on Human Rights (Vienna, Austria, 14–25 June 1993), 171 States reaffirmed that the Universal Declaration "constitutes a common standard of achievement for all peoples and all nations" and that "it is the duty of States, regardless of their political, economic and cultural systems, to promote and protect all human rights and fundamental freedoms."

The Conenants, unlike the Universal Declaration are legally binding treaties for those states which are parties to them and thus are obliged to respect the procedures for their implementation.

STRENGTHENING THE HUMAN RIGHTS MACHINERY: UNITED NATIONS HIGH COMMISSIONER FOR HUMAN RIGHTS

With a view to strengthening the human rights machinery, the UN created the post of UN High Commissioner for Human Rights on December 20, 1993.

Operating under the direction and authority of the Secretary General as his representative in the field of human rights, the High Commissioner also reports to the General Assembly.

The Office of the United Nations High Commissioner for Human Rights (OHCHR) serves as the Secretariat of the Commission on Human Rights, the treaty bodies and other United Nations human rights organs and is the focal point for all United Nations human rights activities.

Human rights activities in the United Nations are coordinated by the Office of the High Commissioner for Human Rights in Geneva. The Office services the UN Commission on Human Rights and most UN human rights treaty bodies. Every year, the Office receives about 400,000 complaints of human rights violations.

People who feel their rights have been violated and are in need of urgent assistance can dial a 24-hour fax hot-line in Geneva:

The Office also maintains a human rights database to help it respond to unresolved or developing situations which may require follow-up and preventive action.

The High Commissioner's work has four essential components:

- Building global partnerships for human rights.
- Preventing human rights violations and responding to emergencies.
- Promoting human rights, together with democracy and development, as the guiding principles for lasting peace.
- Coordinating the system—wide strengthening of the United Nations human rights programmes.

In 1997, the human rights programme of the United Nations was fundamentally restructured in order to strengthen its impact on the coordination of human rights activities throughout the system. The Secretary-General merged the High Commissioner's Office and the former Centre for Human Rights into a single human rights programme, the Office of the United Nations High Commissioner for Human Rights.

Three branches of the High Commissioner's Office now perform the functional activities of the former Centre for Human Rights: the Research and Right to Development Branch, the Support Services Branch and the Activities and Programmes Branch.

The *Research and Right to Development Branch* is involved in all activities related to the promotion and protection of the right to development, in particular by supporting the working groups on the realisation of the right to development, and is also responsible for carrying out research projects. It also supports all thematic mandates and the work of the Sub-commission on Prevention of Discrimination and Protection of Minorities.

The *Support Services Branch* serves as a secretariat to the six treaty bodies, the voluntary funds and to the Commission on Human Rights and its subsidiary bodies. It also processes the hundreds of thousands of complaints from individuals addressed to the United Nations each year.

The *Activities and Programmes Branch* coordinates all Advisory Services and Technical Cooperation Projects and the human rights field offices worldwide. It manages the Voluntary Funds for Advisory Services and Technical Cooperation Projects and for Field Presences, and is responsible for implementing the Plan of Action for the Decade for Human Rights Education. The Branch provides support to the Special Rapporteurs of the Commission on Human Rights, and maintains country desk offices dealing with the human rights situation in specific countries.

UNITED NATIONS LANDMARKS IN HUMAN RIGHTS: A BRIEF CHRONOLOGY

26 June 1945	Signing of the *Charter of the United Nations* and the *Statute of the International Court of justice*, in San Francisco.
21 June 1946	The Economic and Social Council (ECOSOC) establishes the *Commission on Human Rights* and the *Commission on the Status of Women*.

9 December 1948	The General Assembly adopts the *Convention on the Prevention and Punishment of the Crime of Genocide* (entered into force 1951).
10 December 1948	The General Assembly adopts the *Universal Declaration of Human Rights.*
12 August 1949	The Diplomatic Conference for the Establishment of International Conventions for the Protection of Victims of War adopts four *Geneva Conventions,* relating to the Amelioration of the Condition of Wounded and Sick Members of Armed Forces in the Field and at Sea, the Treatment of Prisoners of War and the Protection of Civilians in Wartime (into force 1950).
20 December 1952	The General Assembly adopts the *Convention on the Political Rights of Women* (into force 1954).
1 August 1956	ECOSOC calls for periodic reports (every three years) on human rights and studies of specific rights or groups of rights. This resolution represents the first call for reports from Member States, and was a precursor to the reporting requirements contained in the many subsequent human rights covenants.
20 November 1959	The General Assembly adopts the *Declaration of the Rights of the Child* (see also 20 November 1989).
21 December 1965	The General Assembly adopts the *International Convention on the Elimination of All Forms of Racial Discrimination* (into force 1969). This Convention provides for the

	establishment of the Committee on the Elimination of Racial Discrimination.
16 December 1966	The General Assembly adopts the *International Covenant on Economic, Social and Cultural Rights* (into force 3 January 1976) and the *International Covenant on Civil and Political Rights* with an *Optional Protocol* (into force 23 March 1976). This Covenant provides for the establishment of the Human Rights Committee (see also 28 May 1985).
6 June 1967	ECOSOC adopts *resolution 1235 (XLII)*, authorising the Commission on Human Rights and the Sub-commission on Prevention of Discrimination and Protection of Minorities to examine information relevant to gross violations of human rights and fundamental freedoms.
7 November 1967	The General Assembly adopts the *Declaration on the Elimination of Discrimination against Women*.
13 May 1968	The International Conference on Human Rights adopts the *Proclamation of Tehran*.
26 November 1968	The General Assembly adopts the *Convention on the Non-Applicability of Statutory Limitations to War Crimes against Humanity* (into force 1970).
11 December 1969	The General Assembly adopts the *Declaration on Social Progress and Development*.
30 November 1973	The General Assembly adopts the International Convention on the Suppression and Punishment of the Crime of Apartheid (into force 1976).
9 December 1975	The General Assembly adopts the

	Declaration on the Protection of All Persons from Being Subjected to Torture and Other Cruel, Inhuman or Degrading Treatment or Punishment.
23 March 1976	With entry into force of the *International Covenant on Civil and Political Rights* and the *International Covenant on Economic, Social and Cultural Rights,* 10 years after being originally opened for signature (see 16 December 1966), the *International Bill of Human Rights* becomes a reality (see also 10 December 1948).
18 December 1979	The General Assembly adopts the *Convention on the Elimination of All Forms of Discrimination against Women* (into force 1981). The Convention provides for the establishment of the Committee on the Elimination of Discrimination against Women.
25 November 1981	The General Assembly adopts the *Declaration on the Elimination of All Forms of Intolerance and of Discrimination Based on Religion or Belief.*
10 December 1984	The General Assembly adopts the *Convention against Torture and Other Cruel, Inhuman or Degrading Treatment or Punishment* (into force 1987). The Convention provides for the establishment of the Committee against Torture.
28 May 1985	ECOSOC establishes the *Committee on Economic, Social and Cultural Rights,* responsible for monitoring the implementation of the *International Covenant on Economic, Social and Cultural Rights.*
4 December 1986	The General Assembly adopts the *Declaration on the Right to Development.*

9 December 1988	The General Assembly adopts the *Body of Principles for the Protection of All Persons under Any Form of Detention or Imprisonment*.
24 May 1989	ECOSOC adopts the *Principles on the Effective Prevention and Investigation of Extralegal, Arbitrary and Summary Executions*.
20 November 1989	The General Assembly adopts the *Convention on the Rights of the Child* (into force 1990). The Convention provides for the establishment of the Committee on the Rights of the Child.
18 December 1990	The General Assembly adopts the *International Convention on the Protection of the Rights of All Migrant Workers and Members of Their Families*.
18 December 1992	The General Assembly adopts the *Declaration on the Rights of Persons Belonging to National or Ethnic, Religions and Linguistic Minorities*.
25 May 1993	The Security Council adopts resolution 827 (1993), establishing an *International Criminal Tribunal for the Prosecution of Persons Responsible for Serious Violations of International Humanitarian Law Committed in the Territory of the Former Yugoslavia since 1991*, with its seat at The Hague in the Netherlands.
25 June 1993	The World Conference on Human Rights adopts the *Vienna Declaration and Programme of Action*.
20 December 1993	The General Assembly adopts resolution 48/141, establishing the post of *United Nations High Commissioner for Human Rights*.
5 April 1994	Mr. Jose Ayala Lasso of Ecuador assumes the post of first *United Nations*

	High Commissioner for Human Rights.
8 November 1994	The Security Council adopts resolution 955 (1994), establishing an *International Criminal Tribunal for the Prosecution of Persons Responsible for Genocide and Other Serious Crimes against Humanitarian Law Committed in Rwanda during 1994,* with its seat in Arusha, Tanzania.
23 December 1994	The General Assembly proclaims the *United Nations Decade for Human Rights Education (1995–2004).*
12 September 1997	Ms. Mary Robinson of Ireland becomes the second *United Nations High Commissioner for Human Rights.*
17 July 1998	The Diplomatic Conference of Plenipotentiaries adopts the *Rome Statute of the International Criminal Court,* establishing the International Criminal Court, with its seat at The Hague.
1995–2005	
April 2004	United Nations Decade for Human Rights.
	The UN Commission on Human Rights recommends to the UN General Assembly a plan of action on human rights education focusing on the primary and secondary school system.

Source: *Human Rights Today*, UN Briefing Papers, 1998, UNO.

2

Educational Implications of Human Rights

EDUCATION IN THE DECLARATION OF HUMAN RIGHTS

Education has been specified as one of the fundamental human rights vide Article 26 of the 'Universal Declaration of Human Rights' follows:

Article 26 (i) "Everyone has the right to education. Education shall be free, at least in the elementary and fundamental stages. Technical and professional education shall be equally accessible to all on the basis of merit."

(ii) "Education shall be directed to the full development of the human personality and to the strengthening of respect for human rights and fundamental freedoms."

It shall promote understanding, tolerance and friendship among all nation, racial or religious groups and shall further the activities of the United Nations for the maintenance of peace."

(iii) "Parents have a prior right to choose the kind of education that shall be given to their children.

UNIVERSALISING EDUCATION

There is a close correlation between poverty among families, communities and entire countries, and low levels of education among children, and identifying financial obstacles to universal primary education is the crucial first step towards their elimination. This is mandated by universal human rights standards that assert primary education should be free and compulsory.

International human rights law asserts the public

responsibility for ensuring free and compulsory primary education. Key provisions included in the treaties are summarised below reflecting changes in international human rights law over the last few decades. These changes have reaffirmed that compulsory education should remain free.

KEY TREATY PROVISIONS ON FREE AND COMPULSORY EDUCATION

Universal Declaration of Human Rights (1948). Education shall be free, at least in the elementary and fundamental stages. Elementary education shall be compulsory.

European Convention on Human Rights, Protocol 1 (1952). No person shall be denied the right to education.

UNESCO Convention against Discrimination in Education (1960). The States Parties to this Convention undertake to formulate, develop and apply a national policy which... will tend to promote equality of opportunity and of treatment... and in particular: a) to make primary education free and compulsory.

International Covenant on Economic, Social and Cultural Rights (1966). Primary education shall be compulsory and available free for all.

Protocol of San Salvador to the American Convention on Human Rights (1988). The States Parties to this Protocol recognise that in order to achieve the full exercise of the right to education: a) Primary education should be compulsory and accessible to all without cost.

Convention on the Rights of the Child (1989). States Parties recognise the right of the child to education, and with a view to achieving this right progressively and on the basis of equal opportunity, they shall, in particular: a) make primary education compulsory and available free for all.

Charter on the Rights and Welfare of the African Child (1990). States Parties to the present Charter shall take all appropriate measures with a view to achieving the full realisation of [the right to education] and shall in particular: a) provide free and compulsory basic education.

(Revised) European Social Charter (1996). With a view to ensuring the effective exercise of the right of children and young persons to grow up in an environment which encourages the full development of their personality and of their physical and mental capacities, the Parties undertake, either directly or in co-operation with public and private organisations, to take all appropriate and necessary measures designed:... to provide to children and young persons a free primary and secondary education as well as to encourage regular attendance at schools.

LENGTH OF YEARS OF FREE AND COMPULSORY EDUCATION

UNESCO has compiled data on the length of compulsory education and these provide a useful global overview (Table 2.1). While education is compulsory in most countries in the world, the difference in length from four years at one extreme to 13 at the other reflects the varying willingness and ability of governments to ensure that all children and young people complete a determined length of schooling.

The rights of the child entered international law with the Convention on the Rights of the Child introduced in 1989.

Table 2.1: Legally Mandated Length of Compulsory Education

Years	*Country*
13	Netherlands.
12	Belgium, Brunei Darussalam, Germany, St Kitts and Nevis.
11	Antigua and Barbuda, Armenia, Azerbaijan, Barbados, British Virgin Islands, Dominica, Grenada, Israel, Kazakhstan, Malta, Moldova, United Kingdom.
10	Argentina, Australia, Belize, Canada, Congo, Costa Rica, Dominican Republic, Democratic People's Republic of Korea, Ecuador, France, Gabon, Hungary, Iceland, Kyrgyzstan, Liberia, Monaco, Namibia, New Zealand, Norway, Seychelles, Spain, St. Lucia, St. Vincent and the Grenadines, Venezuela, USA.
9	Algeria, Austria, Bahamas, Bahrain, Belarus, Cambodia, China, Comoros, Cook Islands, Cuba, Cyprus, Czech Republic, Denmark, El Salvador, Estonia, Finland, Georgia, Greece, Hong Kong, Indonesia, Ireland, Japan, Jordan, Kiribati, Lebanon, Libya, Lithuania, Luxembourg, Mali, Netherlands Antilles, Portugal, Republic of Korea, Russia, Sierra Leone, Slovakia, South Africa, Sri Lanka, Sweden, Switzerland, Tajikistan, Tunisia, Ukraine, Yemen.

8	Albania, Angola, Bolivia, Brazil, Bulgaria, Chile, Croatia, Egypt, Fiji, FYROM, Ghana, Guyana, India, Italy, Kenya, Kuwait, Latvia, Malawi, Mongolia, Niger, Poland, Romania, Samoa, San Marino, Slovenia, Somalia, Sudan, Tonga, Turkey, Yugoslavia, Zimbabwe.
7	Burkina Faso, Eritrea, Lesotho, Mauritius, Mozambique, Swaziland, Tanzania, Trinidad and Tobago, Tuvalu, Zambia.
6	Afghanistan, Benin, Burundi, Cameroon, Cape Verde, Central African Republic, Chad, Cote d'Ivoire, Djibouti, Ethiopia, Guatemala, Guinea, Guinea-Bissau, Haiti, Honduras, Iraq, Jamaica, Madagascar, Mauritania, Mexico, Morocco, Nicaragua, Nigeria, Panama, Paraguay, Peru, Philippines, Rwanda, Senegal, Suriname, Syria, Thailand, Togo, United Arab Emirates, Uruguay, Vanuatu.
5	Bangladesh, Colombia, Equatorial Guinea, Iran, Laos, Macao, Myanmar, Nepal, Vietnam.
4	Sao Tome and Principe.

PARENTAL FREEDOM OF CHOICE OF EDUCATING THEIR CHILDREN

The right to education by its very nature requires regulation by the State because the State is responsible for ensuring that all educational institutions comply with prescribed standards. The exercise of parental freedom of choice in educating their children generates a variety of schools, and these standards ought to be observed in them all so as to safeguard education as a public good as well as to protect children against abuse.

4A STRUCTURE OR SCHEME OF EDUCATION

A *'Manual on Rights – Based Education'* published by Asia and Pacific Regional Bureau for Education, Bangkok (2004), details the legal obligations of the governments stemming from the right to education according to the following 4A Scheme.

Availability refers to three different kinds of governmental obligation: education as a civil and political right requires governments to permit the establishment of schools respecting freedom *of* and *in* education; education as a social and economic right requires governments to ensure that free and compulsory education is available to all school-age children; education as a cultural right, meanwhile, requires respect of diversity, expressed in particular through minority and indigenous rights.

Table 2.2: Universal Guarantees for Parental Freedom of Choice: UN Action

Universal Declaration (1948)	Parents have a prior right to choose the kind of education that shall be given to their children.
UNESCO Convention against Discrimination in Education (1960)	The States Parties to this Convention agree that: (b) It is essential to respect the liberty of parents, ... firstly to choose for their children institutions other than those maintained by the public authorities but conforming to... minimum educational standards, and secondly, to ensure...the religious and moral education of the children in conformity with their own convictions.
International Covenant on Economic, Social and Cultural Rights (1966)	The States Parties to the present Covenant undertake to have respect for the liberty of parents...to choose for their children schools, other than those established by the public authorities, which conform to such minimum educational standards as may be laid down or approved by the State and to ensure the religious and moral education of their children in conformity with their own convictions. No part of this article shall be construed so as to interfere with the liberty of individuals and bodies to establish and direct educational institutions ...
International Covenant on Civil and Political Rights (1966)	The States Parties to the present Covenant undertake to have respect for the liberty of parents...to ensure the religious and moral education of their children in conformity with their own convictions.
Convention on the Rights of the Child (1989)	No part of [Articles 28 and 29] shall be construed so as to interfere with the liberty of individuals and bodies to establish and direct educational institutions...

Table 2.3: Minimum School Leaving Age in Asia-Pacific Countries

Country	*School Leaving Age*
Bangladesh	10
Brunei	(not compulsory)
Cambodia	no minimum
Fiji	no minimum
India	14
Indonesia	15
Japan	15
Laos	10
Myanmar	no minimum
Pakistan	(not compulsory)
Papua New Guinea	(not compulsory)
Philippines	12
Republic of Korea	15
Singapore	16
Solomon Islands	(not compulsory)
Sri Lanka	14
Thailand	16
Vietnam	10

Accessibility means governments must strive for the practical elimination of gender and racial discrimination and ensure the equal enjoyment of all human rights, and must not be satisfied with merely formally prohibiting discrimination. In addition, accessibility relates to the primary, secondary and tertiary levels of education in different ways; governments are only obliged to provide access to free and compulsory education for all children in the compulsory age range. The right to education should be realised progressively, ensuring all-encompassing, free and compulsory education is available as soon as possible, and facilitating access to post-compulsory education as circumstances permit.

Acceptability requires minimum guarantees regarding the quality of education, for example in terms of health and safety or professional requirements for teachers, but it is much wider in scope than this. These guarantees have to be set, monitored and enforced by the Government throughout the education system, whether the institutions are public or private. Acceptability has been considerably broadened through the development of international human rights law: indigenous and minority rights have prioritised the language of instruction, while the prohibition of corporal punishment has transformed methods of instruction and school discipline. The emerging perception of children as subjects with the right *to* education and with rights *in* education has further extended the boundaries of acceptability to include the contents of educational curricula and textbooks, which are increasingly considered from the perspective of human rights.

Adaptability requires that schools respond to the needs of each individual child, in keeping with the Convention on the Rights of the Child. This reverses the traditional approach in which schools expected the children to adapt to whatever form of education the school provided. As human rights do not exist in isolation, adaptability involves safeguarding all human rights *within* education as well as enhancing human rights *through* education. This necessitates cross-sectoral analysis of the impact of education on the whole range of human rights, to monitor, for example, graduate employment by ensuring integrated planning between the relevant sectors.

GLOBAL HUMAN RIGHTS STANDARDS ON LANGUAGE, MINORITY AND INDIGENOUS RIGHTS

UNESCO Convention against Discrimination in Education (1960)

It is essential to recognise the right of members of national minorities to carry out their own educational activities, including the maintenance of schools and, depending on the educational policy of each state, the use or the teaching of their own language, provided however:

(i) That this right is not exercised in a manner which prevents the members of these minorities from understanding the culture and the language of the community as a whole and from participating in its activities, or which prejudices national sovereignty;

(ii) That attendance at such schools is optional.

International Covenant on Civil and Political Rights (1966)

In those States in which ethnic, religious or linguistic minorities exist, persons belonging to such minorities shall not be denied the right, in community with other members of their group, to enjoy their own culture, to profess and practise their own religion, or to use their own language.

ILO Indigenous and Tribal Peoples Convention (1989)

Measures shall be taken to ensure that members of the [indigenous and tribal] people have the opportunity to acquire education at all levels on at least an equal footing with the rest of the national community. Education programmes and services for the [indigenous and tribal] people shall be developed and implemented in cooperation with them...

In addition, governments should recognise the right of these people to establish their own educational institutions and facilities, provided that such institutions meet minimum standards established by the competent authority in consultation with these peoples. Appropriate resources shall be provided for this purpose.

Children belonging to the [indigenous and tribal] people whenever practicable, be taught to read and write in their own language or in the language most commonly used by the group to which they belong. When this is not practicable, the competent authorities shall undertake consultations with these people with a view to the adoption of measures to achieve this objective.

Adequate measures shall be taken to ensure that these people have the opportunity to attain fluency in the national language or in one of the official languages of the country.

Convention on the Rights of the Child (1989)

In those States in which ethnic, religious or linguistic minorities or persons of indigenous origin exist, a child belonging to such a minority or who is indigenous shall not be denied the right, in community with other members of his or her group, to enjoy his or her own culture, to profess and practise his or her own religion, or to use his or her own language.

HUMAN RIGHTS REQUIREMENTS AND CONTENTS (CURRICULUM) OF EDUCATION

All human rights treaties include specific guidelines for developing the contents of education. The key provisions are given as under:

UNESCO Convention against Discrimination in Education (1960)

The States Parties to this Convention agree that: (a) Education shall be directed to the full development of the human personality and to the strengthening of respect for human rights and fundamental freedoms; it shall promote understanding, tolerance and friendship among all nations, racial and religious groups, and shall further the activities of the United Nations for the maintenance of peace.

International Convention on the Elimination of All Forms of Racial Discrimination (1965)

States Parties undertake to adopt immediate and effective measures, particularly in the fields of teaching, education, culture and information, with a view to combating prejudices which lead to racial discrimination and to promoting understanding, tolerance and friendship among nations and racial or ethnical groups, as well as to propagating the purposes and principles of the Charter of the United Nations, the Universal Declaration of Human Rights, the United Nations Declaration on the Elimination of All Forms of Racial Discrimination, and this Convention.

International Covenant on Economic, Social and Cultural Rights (1966)

The States Parties to the present Covenant... agree that education shall be directed to the full development of the human personality and the sense of its dignity, and shall strengthen the respect for human rights and fundamental freedoms. They further agree that education shall enable all persons to participate effectively in a free society, promote understanding, tolerance and friendship among all nations and all racial, ethnic or religious groups, and further the activities of the United Nations for the maintenance of peace...

Convention on the Elimination of All Forms of Discrimination against Women (1979)

States Parties shall take all appropriate measures to eliminate discrimination against women in order to ensure to them equal rights with men in the field of education and in particular to ensure, on the basis of equality of men and women... (c). The elimination of any stereotyped concept of the roles of men and women at all levels and in all forms of education by encouraging co-education and other types of education which will help to achieve this aim and, in particular, by the revision of textbooks and school programmes and the adaptation of teaching methods...

ILO Indigenous and Tribal Peoples Convention (1989)

The imparting of general knowledge and skills that will help children belonging to the [indigenous and tribal] people to participate fully and on an equal footing in their own community and in the national community shall be the aim of education for these people.

Educational measures shall be taken among all sections of the national community, and particularly among those that are in most direct contact with the [indigenous and tribal] people with the object of eliminating prejudices that they may harbour in respect of these people. To this end, efforts shall be made that history textbooks and other educational materials provide a fair, accurate and informative portrayal of the societies and cultures of these people.

Convention on the Rights of the Child (1989)

States Parties agree that the education of the child shall be directed to: (a) The development of the child's personality, talents and mental and physical abilities to their fullest potential; (b) The development of respect for human rights and fundamental freedoms, and for the principles enshrined in the Charter of the United Nations; (c) The development of respect for the child's parents, his or her own cultural identity, language and values, for the national values of the country in which the child is living, the country from which he or she may originate and for civilisations different from his or her own; (d) The preparation of the child for responsible life in a free society, in the spirit of understanding, peace, tolerance, equality of sexes, and friendship among all peoples, ethnic, national and religious groups and persons of indigenous origin; (e) The development of respect for the natural environment.

3

Human Rights and Indian Constitutional Provisions

DECLARATION HUMAN RIGHTS AND FUNDAMENTAL RIGHTS

A personal of the Constitution of India shows that though the term 'Human Rights' is not used, the inclusion of 'Fundamental Rights' denotes the same intention and meaning as inherent in The Declaration of Human Rights. It is, therefore, important that we may apprise ourselves of the various dimensions of Fundamental Rights.

MEANING OF FUNDAMENTAL RIGHTS

Fundamental rights are those legal rights which are framed not by the Legislature but are provided for in the Constitution of India.

The rights are fundamental on account of four reasons.

First, they are included in the Constitution which is known as the 'Fundamental Law of the Land.'

Second, they are justiciable. The Supreme Court and the High Courts have the power to enforce whenever these rights are violated.

Third, the rights are held to be belonging to all citizens, irrespective of caste, creed, race, religion, sex etc.

Fourth, they are indispensable to the all round development of the personality of an individual.

In the words of Dr. S.C. Kashyap and Vishva Prakash, "Whereas the ordinary rights can be changed by legislature through simple law making process, the fundamental rights cannot be changed easily."

SIGNIFICANCE AND NEED FOR FUNDAMENTAL RIGHTS AS INCLUDED IN OUR CONSTITUTION (PART III ARTICLES 14 TO 32)

Justice Gandragadkar has described the inclusion of fundamental rights in our Constitution as "the very foundation and cornerstone of the democratic way of life ushered in this country by the Constitution." (Sajjan Singh vs. State of Rajasthan, AIR 1965 SC 845).

In the words of *Justice Bhagwati*, "These fundamental rights represent the basic values cherished by the people of this country since the Vedic times and they are calculated to protect the dignity of the individual and create conditions in which every human being can develop his personality to the fullest extent. They weave a 'pattern of guarantee' in the basic structure of human rights and impose negative obligations on the State not to encroach on individual liberty in its various dimensions. (Maneka Gandhi vs. Union of India, AIR 1978, SC 597)

Dr. S. Radhakrishnan considers the fundamental rights "as a pledge to our people and a pact with the civilised world."

Justice Patanjali has said, "The whole object of Part III of the Constitution is to provide protection for the freedoms and rights mentioned therein against arbitrary invasion by the State (State of West Bengal vs. Subodh Gopal Bose, AIR 1954, SC 1992).

Dr. B.R. Ambedkar described fundamental rights as "the heart and soul of the Constitution."

The importance of these rights is brought out as under:

1. *Necessary for the Optimum Development of Individuals*. The rights such as right of equality, freedom of religion etc., help in the development of inherent strength of an individual in a democratic country like India.
2. *Essential in a Democratic Set-up*. In a democratic set-up, people choose their own government. For fair reflection of opinion, people need to have certain freedoms which are granted to them through the fundamental rights.
3. *Essential for a Multi-Cultural and Multi-Religious Society*. India is a vast country having people belonging to different religions and cultures. For national unity, it is

required that all people should be free to profess the religion of their choice. There should not be any discrimination on the part of government on grounds of religion, race, sex etc. This is ensured by the fundamental rights available to the citizens.

4. *Check on the Arbitrary Power of the Executive and Legislature.* The inclusion of fundamental rights in the Constitution protects the citizens on the arbitrary power of the government.
5. *Establishment of Social Democracy.* Articles 15 and 16 prohibit discrimination on the grounds of religion, race, caste, sex or birth.
6. *Protection of the Interest of the Minorities.* The fundamental rights provide for safeguarding the language, script and education of the minorities.
7. *Promotion of Education.* Education is considered as an instrument of peaceful revolution in different areas of life of the individual as well of the society. Realising this, 'Right to Education' has been included as Fundamental right by the Eighty-Sixth Amendment to the Constitution introduced in 2002 under Article 21A.
8. *Fundamental Unity of India.* By providing the same liberties, irrespective of social status, wealth, race, caste, sex and place of birth, to all, the Constitution emphasis the national unity of India.

ORIGIN AND DEVELOPMENT OF THE CONCEPT OF FUNDAMENTAL RIGHTS

In India, the plea for granting Fundamental Rights to the Indians by the British rulers was first made by Dadabhai Naoroji (1825–1917), one of the foremost reformers of all kinds—educational, political, religious and social and who became the president of the Indian National Congress three times, in 1886, 1894 and 1906. The Karachi session (1931) of the Indian National Congress drafted the model for Fundamental Rights. However, the dream materialised only when India achieved its independence and the Constitution included Fundamental Rights.

NATURE AND MAIN FEATURES OF FUNDAMENTAL RIGHTS

1. The rights form an integral part of the Constitution.
2. Fundamental rights are justifiable. In case of violation, one can seek protection.
3. These rights are available not only to citizens, but in certain cases to the foreigners living in India too; for instance right to religion.
4. The rights are not absolute. Each right is given under certain limitations and reasonable restrictions are also provided for.
5. Some rights are positive in nature like right to liberty or religion.
6. Some rights are negative in nature, e.g., abolition of untouchability.
7. Fundamental rights can be amended or even deleted but for this an elaborate process is needed.
8. Rights are liable to suspension. During Emergency, fundamental rights can be suspended.
9. Fundamental rights are comprehensive in nature.
10. Fundamental rights differentiate between citizens and persons. For instance freedom of speech and expression, freedom of movement are secured only to citizens while the rights relating to the protection of life and personal liberty are granted to every person irrespective of his or her being a citizen of India.
11. Fundamental rights definitely stand on a higher pedestal than the ordinary laws.
12. Fundamental rights put restrictions on the powers of the State also. If the State violates these rights, the citizens can seek redress through the courts.
13. Rights limit the authority of the Government.

CLASSIFICATION OF FUNDAMENTAL RIGHTS AND THEIR DESCRIPTION

- Right to Equality
- Right to Freedom
- Right against Exploitation
- Right to Freedom of Religion

- Cultural and Educational Rights
- Right to Constitutional Remedies.

Articles: Constitution of India and Articles Relating to Fundamental Rights

Part III of the Constitution of India entitled 'Fundamental Rights' includes 24 Articles — 12 to 35. Article 12 relates to the definition of the word 'State' and Article 13 to Laws inconsistence with or in derogation of the Fundamental Rights. Article 34 provides for restrictions on rights while martial law is in force. Article 35 deals with legislation to give effect to provisions of this part.

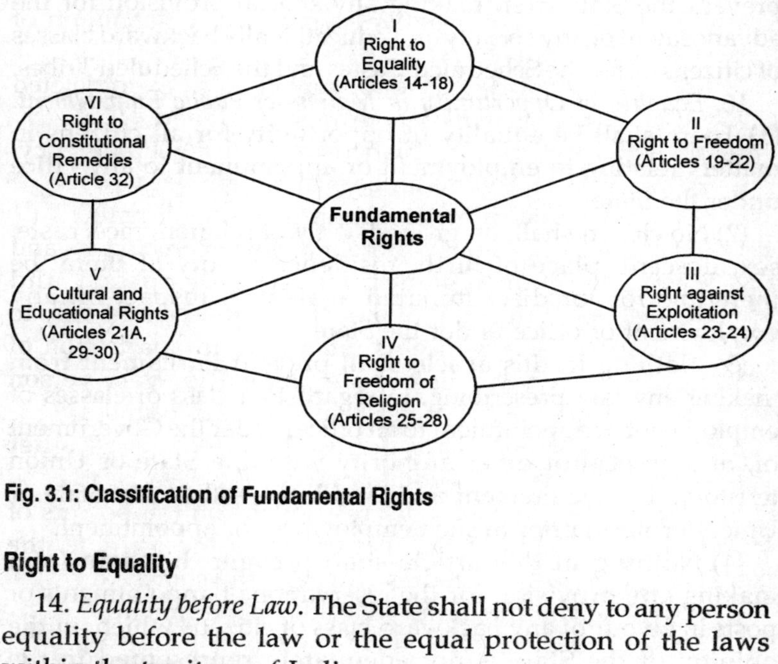

Fig. 3.1: Classification of Fundamental Rights

Right to Equality

14. *Equality before Law.* The State shall not deny to any person equality before the law or the equal protection of the laws within the territory of India.

15. *Prohibition of Discrimination on Grounds of Religion, Race, Caste, Sex or Place of Birth.* (1) The State shall not discriminate against any citizen on grounds only of religion, race, caste, sex, place of birth or any of them. (2) No citizen shall, on grounds only of religion, race, caste, sex, place of birth or any of them, be subject to any disability, liability, restriction or condition

with regard to—

(a) access to shops, public restaurants, hotels and places of public entertainment; or
(b) the use of wells, tanks, bathing ghats, roads and places of public resort maintained wholly or partly out of State funds or dedicated to the use of the general public.

(3) Nothing in this article shall prevent the State from making any special provision for women and children.

(4) Nothing in this article or in clause (2) of Article 29 shall prevent the State from making any special provision for the advancement of any socially and educationally backward classes of citizens or for the Scheduled Castes and the Scheduled Tribes.

16. *Equality of Opportunity in Matters of Public Employment.* (1) There shall be equality of opportunity for all citizens in matters relating to employment or appointment to any office under the State.

(2) No citizen shall, on grounds only of religion, race, caste, sex, descent, place of birth, residence or any of them, be ineligible for, or discriminated against in respect of, any employment or office under the State.

(3) Nothing in this article shall prevent Parliament from making any law prescribing, in regard to a class or classes of employment or appointment to an office (under the Government of, or any local or other authority within, a State or Union territory, any requirement as to residence within that State or Union territory) prior to such employment or appointment.

(4) Nothing in this article shall prevent the State from making any provision for the reservation of appointments or posts in favour of any backward class of citizens which, in the opinion of the State is not adequately represented in the services under the State.

4(A) Nothing in this article shall prevent the State from making any provision for reservation (in matters of promotion, with consequential seniority, to any class) or classes of posts in the services under the State in favour of the Scheduled Castes and the Scheduled Tribes which in the opinion of the State are not adequately represented in the services under the State.

4(B) Nothing in this article shall prevent the State from considering any unfilled vacancies of a year which are reserved for being filled up in that year in accordance with any provision for reservation made under clause (4) or clause 4(A) as a separate class of vacancies to be filled up in any succeeding year or years and such class of vacancies shall not be considered together with the vacancies of the year in which they are being filled up for determining the ceiling of fifty per cent, reservation on total number of vacancies of that year.

(5) Nothing in this article shall affect the operation of any law which provides that the incumbent of an office in connection with the affairs of any religious or denominational institution or any member of the governing body thereof shall be a person professing a particular religion or belonging to a particular denomination.

17. *Abolition of Untouchability.* "Untouchability" is abolished and its practice in any form is forbidden. The enforcement of any disability rising out of "Untouchability" shall be an offence punishable in accordance with law.

18. *Abolition of Titles.* (1) No title, not being a military or academic distinction, shall be conferred by the State.

(2) No citizen of India shall accept any title from any foreign State.

(3) No person who is not a citizen of India shall, while he holds any office of profit or trust under the State, accept without the consent of the President any title from any foreign State.

(4) No person holding any office of profit or trust under the State shall, without the consent of the President, accept any present, emolument, or office of any kind from or under any foreign State.

Right to Freedom

19. *Protection of Certain Rights Regarding Freedom of Speech, etc.* (1) All citizens shall have the right—

(a) to freedom of speech and expression;

(b) to assemble peaceably and without arms;

(c) to form associations or unions;

(d) to move freely throughout the territory of India;

(e) to reside and settle in any part of the territory of India; and

(g) to practise any profession, or to carry on any occupation, trade or business.

(2) Nothing in sub-clause (a) of clause (1) shall affect the operation of any existing law, or prevent the State from making any law, in so far as such law imposes reasonable restrictions on the exercise of the right conferred by the said sub-clause in the interests of the sovereignty and integrity of India, the security of the State, friendly relations with Foreign States, public order, decency or morality, or in relation to contempt of court, defamation or incitement to an offence.

(3) Nothing in sub-clause (b) of the said clause shall affect the operation of any existing law in so far as it imposes, or prevents the State from making any law imposing, in the interests of the sovereignty and integrity of India or public order, reasonable restrictions on the exercise of the right conferred by the said sub-clause.

(4) Nothing in sub-clause (c) of the said clause shall affect the operation of any existing law in so far as it imposes, or prevents the State from making any law imposing, in the interests of the sovereignty and integrity of India or public order or morality, reasonable restrictions on the exercise of the right conferred by the said sub-clause.

(5) Nothing in sub-clauses (d) and (e) of the said clause shall affect the operation of any existing law in so far as it imposes, or prevents the State from making any law imposing, reasonable restrictions on the exercise of any of the rights conferred by the said sub-clauses either in the interests of the general public or for the protection of the interests of any Scheduled Tribe.

(6) Nothing in sub-clause (g) of the said clause shall affect the operation of any existing law in so far as it imposes, or prevents the State from making any law imposing, in the interests of the general public, reasonable restrictions on the exercise of the right conferred by the said sub-clause, and, in particular, nothing in the said sub-clause shall affect the

operation of any existing law in so far as it relates to, or prevents the State from making any law relating to,—

(i) the professional or technical qualifications necessary for practising any profession or carrying on any occupation, trade or business, or

(ii) the carrying on by the State, or by a corporation owned or controlled by the State, of any trade, business, industry or service, whether to the exclusion, complete or partial, of citizens or otherwise.

20. *Protection in Respect of Conviction for Offences.* (1) No person shall be convicted of any offence except for violation of a law in force at the time of the commission of the act charged as an offence, nor be subjected to a penalty greater than that which might have been inflicted under the law in force at the time of the commission of the offence.

(2) No person shall be prosecuted and punished for the same offence more than once.

(3) No person accused of any offence shall be compelled to be a witness against himself.

21. *Protection of Life and Personal Liberty.* No person shall be deprived of his life or personal liberty except according to procedure established by law.

21A. *Right to Education.* The State shall provide free and compulsory education to all children of the age of six to fourteen years in such manner as the State may, by law, determine.

22. *Protection Against Arrest and Detention in Certain Cases.* (1) No person who is arrested shall be detained in custody without being informed, as soon as may be, of the grounds for such arrest nor shall he be denied the right to consult, and to be defended by, a legal practitioner of his choice.

(2) Every person who is arrested and detained in custody shall be produced before the nearest magistrate within a period of twenty-four hours of such arrest excluding the time necessary for the journey from the place of arrest to the court of the magistrate and no such person shall be detained in custody beyond the said period without the authority of a magistrate.

(3) Nothing in clauses: (1) and (2) shall apply—

(a) to any person who for the time being is an enemy alien; or
(b) to any person who is arrested or detained under any law providing for preventive detention.

(4) No law providing for preventive detention shall authorise the detention of a person for a longer period than three months unless—

(a) an Advisory Board consisting of persons who are, or have been, or are qualified to be appointed as, Judges of a High Court has reported before the expiration of the said period of three months that there is in its opinion sufficient cause for such detention:

Provided that nothing in this sub-clause shall authorise the detention of any person beyond the maximum period prescribed by any law made by Parliament under sub-clause (b) of clause (7); or

(b) such person is detained in accordance with the provisions of any law made by Parliament under sub-clauses (a) and (b) of clause (7).

(5) When any person is detained in pursuance of an order made under any law providing for preventive detention, the authority making the order shall, as soon as may be, communicate to such person the grounds on which the order has been made and shall afford him the earliest opportunity of making a representation against the order.

(6) Nothing in clause (5) shall require the authority making any such order as is referred to in that clause to disclose facts which such authority considers to be against the public interest to disclose.

(7) Parliament may by law prescribe—

(a) the circumstances under which, and the class or classes of cases in which, a person may be detained for a period longer than three months under any law providing for preventive detention without obtaining the opinion of an Advisory Board in accordance with the provisions of sub-clause (a) of clause (4);

(b) the maximum period for which any person may in any class or classes of cases be detained under any law providing for preventive detention; and

(c) the procedure to be followed by an Advisory Board in an inquiry under sub-clause (a) of clause (4).

Right against Exploitation

23. *Prohibition of traffic in Human beings and Forced Labour.* (1) Traffic in human beings and beggar and other similar forms of forced labour are prohibited and any contravention of this provision shall be an offence punishable in accordance with law.

(2) Nothing in this article shall prevent the State from imposing compulsory service for public purposes, and in imposing such service the State shall not make any discrimination on grounds only of religion, race, caste or class or any of them.

24. *Prohibition of Employment of Children in Factories, etc.* No child below the age of fourteen years shall be employed to work in any factory or mine or engaged in any other hazardous employment.

Right to Freedom of Religion

25. *Freedom of Conscience and Free Profession, Practice and Propagation of Religion.* (1) Subject to public order, morality and health and to the other provisions of this Part, all persons are equally entitled to freedom of conscience and the right freely to profess, practise and propagate religion.

(2) Nothing in this article shall affect the operation of any existing law or prevent the State from making any law—

(a) regulating or restricting any economic, financial, political or other secular activity which may be associated with religious practice;

(b) providing for social welfare and reform or the throwing open of Hindu religious institutions of a public character to all classes and sections of Hindus.

Explanation I. The wearing and carrying of kirpans shall be deemed to be included in the profession of the Sikh religion.

Explanation II. In sub-clause (b) of clause (2), the reference to Hindus shall be construed as including a reference to persons professing the Sikh, Jaina or Buddhist religion, and the reference to Hindu religious institutions shall be construed accordingly.

26. *Freedom to Manage Religious Affairs*. Subject to public order, morality and health, every religious denomination or any section thereof shall have the right—

(a) to establish and maintain institutions for religious and charitable purposes;
(b) to manage its own affairs in matters of religion;
(c) to own and acquire movable and immovable property; and
(d) to administer such property in accordance with law.

27. *Freedom as to Payment of Taxes for Promotion of any Particular Religion*. No person shall be compelled to pay any taxes, the proceeds of which are specifically appropriated in payment of expenses for the promotion or maintenance of any particular religion or religious denomination.

28. *Freedom as to Attendance at Religious Instruction or Religious Worship in Certain Educational Institutions*. (1) No religious instruction shall be provided in any educational institution wholly maintained out of State funds.

(2) Nothing in clause; (1) shall apply to an educational institution which is administered by the State but has been established under any endowment or trust which requires that religious instruction shall be imparted in such institution.

(3) No person attending any educational institution recognised by the State or receiving aid out of State funds shall be required to take part in any religious instruction that may be imparted in such institution or to attend any religious worship that may be conducted in such institution or in any premises attached thereto unless such person or, if such person is a minor, his guardian has given his consent thereto.

Cultural and Educational Rights

29. *Protection of Interests of Minorities*. (1) Any section of the citizens residing in the territory of India or any part thereof having a distinct language, script or culture of its own shall

have the right to conserve the same.

(2) No citizen shall be denied admission into any educational institution maintained by the State or receiving aid out of State funds on grounds only of religion, race, caste, language or any of them.

30. *Right of Minorities to Establish and Administer Educational Institutions.* (1) All minorities, whether based on religion or language, shall have the right to establish and administer educational institutions of their choice.

(1A) In making any law providing for the compulsory acquisition of any property of any educational institution established and administered by a minority, referred to in clause (1), the State shall ensure that the amount fixed by or determined under such law for the acquisition of such property is such as would not restrict or abrogate the right guaranteed under that clause.

(2) The State shall not, in granting aid to educational institutions, discriminate against any educational institution on the ground that it is under the management of a minority, whether based on religion or language.

31. *Compulsory Acquisition of Property.* [Rep. by the Constitution (Forty-fourth Amendment) Act, 1978, sec. 6 (w.e.f. 20-6-1979)].

31A. *Saving of Laws Providing for Acquisition of Estates, etc.* (1) Notwithstanding anything contained in Article 13, no law providing for—

(a) the acquisition by the State of any estate or of any rights therein or the extinguishment or modification of any such rights, or
(b) the taking over of the management of any property by the State for a limited period either in the public interest or in order to secure the proper management of the property, or
(c) the amalgamation of two or more corporations either in the public interest or in order to secure the proper management of any of the corporations, or
(d) the extinguishment or modification of any rights of managing agents, secretaries and treasurers, managing directors, directors or managers of corporations, or of

any voting rights of shareholders thereof, or

(e) the extinguishment or modification of any rights accruing by virtue of any agreement, lease or licence for the purpose of searching for, or winning, any mineral or mineral oil, or the premature termination or cancellation of any such agreement, lease or licence, shall be deemed to be void on the ground that it is inconsistent with, or takes away or abridges any of the rights conferred by Article 14 or Article 19.

Right to Constitutional Remedies

32. *Remedies for Enforcement of Rights Conferred by this Part.* (1) The right to move the Supreme Court by appropriate proceedings for the enforcement of the rights conferred by this Part is guaranteed.

(2) The Supreme Court shall have power to issue directions or orders or writs, including writs in the nature of *habeas corpus, mandamus,* prohibition, *quo warranto* and certiorari, whichever may be appropriate, for the enforcement of any of the rights conferred by this Part.

(3) Without prejudice to the powers conferred on the Supreme Court by clauses (1) and (2), Parliament may by law empower any other court to exercise within the local limits of its jurisdiction all or any of the powers exercisable by the Supreme Court under clause (2).

(4) The right guaranteed by this article shall not be suspended except as otherwise provided for by this Constitution.

33. *Power of Parliament to Modify the Rights Conferred by this Part in Ttheir Application to Forces, etc.* Parliament may, by law, determine to what extent any of the rights conferred by this Part shall, in their application to,—

(a) the members of the Armed Forces; or
(b) the members of the Forces charged with the maintenance of public order; or
(c) persons employed in any bureau or other organisation established by the State for purposes of intelligence or counter intelligence; or
(d) persons employed in, or in connection with, the telecommunication systems set up for the purposes of

any Force, bureau or organisation referred to in clauses (a) to (c), be restricted or abrogated so as to ensure the proper discharge of their duties and the maintenance of discipline among them.

34. *Restriction on Rights Conferred by this Part While Martial Law is in Force in Any Area.* Notwithstanding anything in the foregoing provisions of this Part, Parliament may by law indemnify any person in the service of the Union or of a State or any other person in respect of any act done by him in connection with the maintenance or restoration of order in any area within the territory of India where martial law was in force or validate any sentence passed, punishment inflicted, forfeiture ordered or other act done under martial law in such area.

35. *Legislation to give effect to the provisions of this Part.* Notwithstanding anything in this Constitution,—

(a) Parliament shall have, and the Legislature of a State shall not have, power to make laws—

(i) with respect to any of the matters which under clause (3) of Article 16, clause (3) of Article 32, Article 33 and Article 34 may be provided for by law made by Parliament; and

(ii) for prescribing punishment for those acts which are declared to be offences under this Part, and Parliament shall, as soon as may be after the commencement of this Constitution, make laws for prescribing punishment for the acts referred to in sub-clause (ii);

(b) Any law in force immediately before the commencement of this Constitution in the territory of India with respect to any of the matters referred to in sub-clause (i) of clause (a) or providing for punishment for any act referred to in sub-clause (ii) of that clause shall, subject to the terms thereof and to any adaptations and modifications that may be made therein under Article 372, continue in force until altered or repealed or amended by Parliament.

17.7 FUNDAMENTAL RIGHTS WITH PROVISIONS AT A GLANCE

Right to Equality	*Right to Freedom*	*Right against Exploitation*	*Right to Freedom of Religion*	*Cultural and Educational Rights of Minorities*	*Right to Edu-cation*	*Right to Consti-tutional Remedies*
1. Equality before law and equal protection before law [Art. 14].	1. Freedom of speech and expression; assembly; association; movement, residence and settlement; profession [Art. 19].	1. Prohibition of traffic in human beings and forced labour [Art. 23].	1. Freedom of conscience and free profession [Art 25].	1. Protection of language, script or culture of minorities [Art. 29].	Article 21A	Remedies for enforcement of the fundamental right conferred by this part,—writs of *habeas corpus*, mandamus, prohibition, certiorari and quo warranto [Art. 32].
2. Prohibition of discrimination on ground of religion etc. [Art. 15].	2. Protection in respect of conviction for offences [Art. 20].	2. Prohibition of employment of children in hazardous employment [Art. 24].	2. Freedom to manage religious affairs [Art. 26].	2. Right of minorities to establish and administer educational institutions [Art. 30].		
3. Equality of opportunity in public employment [Art. 16].	3. Protection of life and personal liberty [Art. 21].		3. Freedom as to payment of taxes for promotion of any particular religion [Art. 27].			
4. Abolition of untouchability [Art. 17].	4. Protection against arrest and detention in certain cases [Art. 22].		4. Freedom as to attendance at religious instruction in certain educational institutions [Art. 28].			
5. Abolition of titles [Art. 18].						

CONSTITUTION OF INDIA AND HUMAN RIGHTS

The Constitution of India incorporates the fundamental values as contained in the UN Declaration of Human Rights. There are several Articles in Part III of the Constitution entitled 'Fundamental Rights' which are quite parallel to the Declaration. Likewise Part IV 'Directive Principles of State Policy' contains several provisions similar to human rights.

Article 14 of the Constitution provides: 'The State shall not deny to any person equality before law." This provision reflects the spirit of Article 2 of the UN Declaration of Human Rights. Article 19 of our Constitution gives every Indian the right to move freely, settle and reside in any part of India. This is commensurate with the Article 13 of the Declaration which provides for freedom of movement and residence.

Other provisions in our Constitution which are parallel to the Declaration of Human Rights include Right of Freedom of Worship and Propagation of Religion (Article 25), Right of Conservation of One's Language and Culture (Article 29); Right of Equal pay for Equal Work for both Men and Women (Article 39) and Right to have Free and Compulsory Education up to the age of 14 (Article 21A).

Fundamental Rights in the Indian Constitution which are by and large, parallel to UN Declaration of Human Rights

UN Declaration of Human Rights		*Indian Constitution and Fundamental Rights*
Article 1	Right to freedom	Article 19
Article 2	Freedom from discrimination	Article 15
Article 3	Right to life, liberty and security of persons	Article 21
Article 5	Freedom from torture or degrading treatment	Article 23
Article 6, 7	Equality before law	Article 14
Article 8	Right to remedy through a competent tribunal	Article 32
Article 9	Freedom from arbitrary arrest	Article 22
Article 13	Right to freedom of movement and residence	Article 19 (d and e)
Article 18	Freedom of belief and religion	Article 25
Article 19	Freedom of opinion and information	Article 19 (a)
Article 20	Right to peaceful assembly and association	Article 19 (b)
Article 26	Right to education	Article 21 (a)
Article 30	Freedom from State or other interference in any of the above rights	Article 32

4

Human Rights Education at Secondary Level: Curriculum and Activities

SIGNIFICANCE AND MEANING OF PROMOTING HUMAN RIGHTS EDUCATION

The United Nations considers education as the key to development, as a fundamental human right and as a prime means in the promotion of human rights. The Universal Declaration of Human Rights Article 26.2 states "Education shall be directed to the full development of the human personality and to the strengthening of respect for human rights and fundamental freedoms. It shall promote understanding, tolerance and friendship among all nations, racial or religious groups and shall further the activities of the United Nations for the maintenance of peace."

In the words of the General Assembly resolution establishing the Decade of Human Rights Education, human rights education is intended to be "a life-long process by which people at all levels of development and in all strata of society learn respect for the dignity of others and the means of ensuring that respect in all societies." In this sense, human rights education significantly contributes to promoting equality and sustainable development, preventing conflict and human rights violations and enhancing participation and democratic processes, with a view to developing societies in which all human rights of all are valued and respected.

According to UNESCO Director-General Koichiro Matsuura, "Human rights education is indispensable for every individual to fully enjoy and claim a life of security and dignity. It is indispensable for public officials to give effect to human rights commitments by the State. Finally, it is indispensable for the entire society to develop and nurture a human rights culture as a prerequisite of harmonious and peaceful development."

Human rights education aims at teaching skills, offering knowledge and shaping attitudes, that advance a universal culture of human rights. While human rights education is a global issue, it is effective primarily at the national level and local levels. It is through human rights education that the standards established in international human rights law take root in the everyday life of individuals and the local culture of nations. The 1993 Vienna Conference — a landmark in human rights education confirmed that human rights education, training and public information were essential for fostering mutual understanding, tolerance and peace among communities.

Human rights education implies that education which enables an individual to understand his rights.

IMPORTANT ASPECTS OF HUMAN RIGHTS EDUCATION

Important aspects of human rights are given below:

- Learning about human rights as an important element of the preparation of all young people for life in a democracy,
- The historical struggle for human rights to be a topic in curriculum,
- The teaching of human rights has to face the problem of the re-emergence of racist attitudes and has to teach the recognition and acceptance of differences,
- Human rights education to take into account the international dimension of the problem,
- Human rights education may have to face the problem of the ideological and political dimension of the human rights debate,
- Human rights education focuses on instances of progress

in the protection of human rights in order to avoid the feeling of discouragement when confronted with the violations of human rights.

BRIEF HISTORY OF HUMAN RIGHTS EDUCATION

In 1974 the General Conference of UNESCO adopted the "Recommendation concerning Education for International Understanding, Cooperation and Peace and Education relating to Human Rights and Fundamental Freedoms" that has gained very large acceptance and has inspired teachers, students and educational authorities as well as peace and human rights activists, individuals and associations, all over the world in their work. In 1978 and 1987 UNESCO held international congresses on human rights teaching, information and documentation in Vienna and Malta resulting in long-term actions of the Organisation. In March 1993 the third Congress in their series was organised in Montreal, Canada, where a World Plan of Action on Education for Human Rights and Democracy was adopted as a common strategy of all those committed to these aims. The United Nations World Conference on Human Rights (Vienna, June 1993) commended as the basis for relevant actions in the future.

In 1994, the United Nations Decade (1995–2004) was proclaimed.

In April 2004, the Commission on Human Rights adopted resolution 2004/71 in which it took note of the need to continue a global framework for human rights education beyond the Decade.

THE THREE DIMENSIONS OF HUMAN RIGHTS EDUCATION

1. To teach about human rights, i.e., to inform people of their rights.
2. To teach for human rights, i.e., to learn how to implement and to defend human rights.
3. To teach in human rights, i.e., to learn within an environment and climate which would reflect a concern for the ideals and practices of human rights.

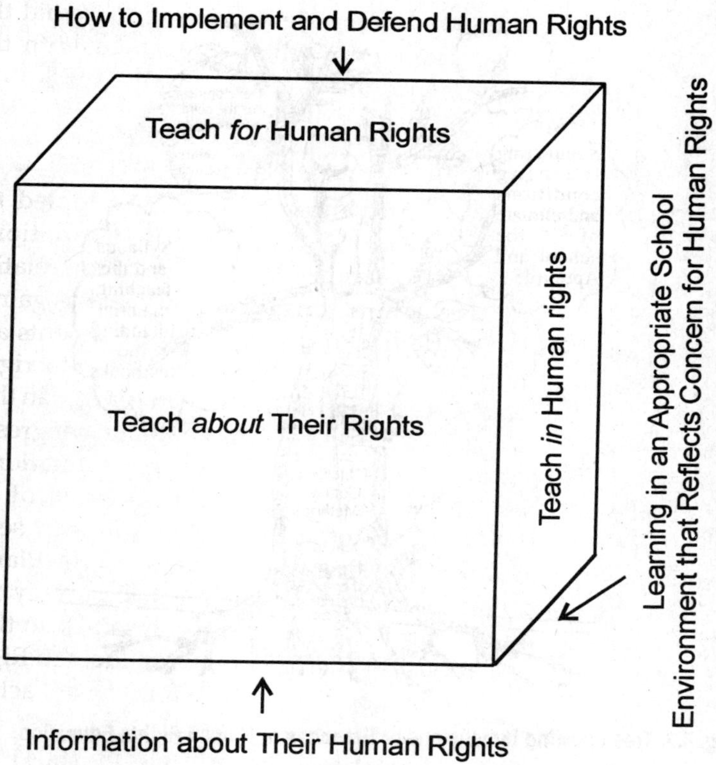

Fig. 4.1: Dimensions of Human Rights Education

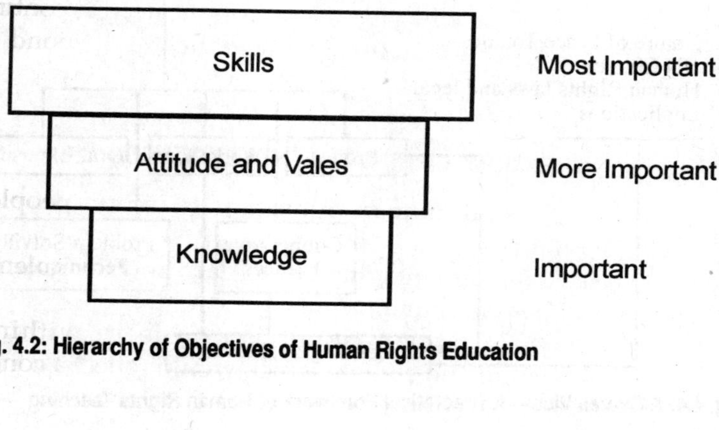

Fig. 4.2: Hierarchy of Objectives of Human Rights Education

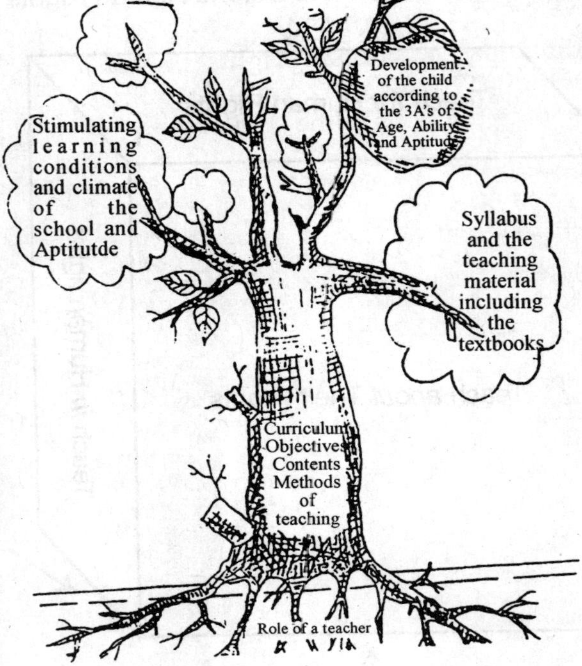

Fig. 4.3: Tree Showing Dimensions or Branches or Human Rights Education

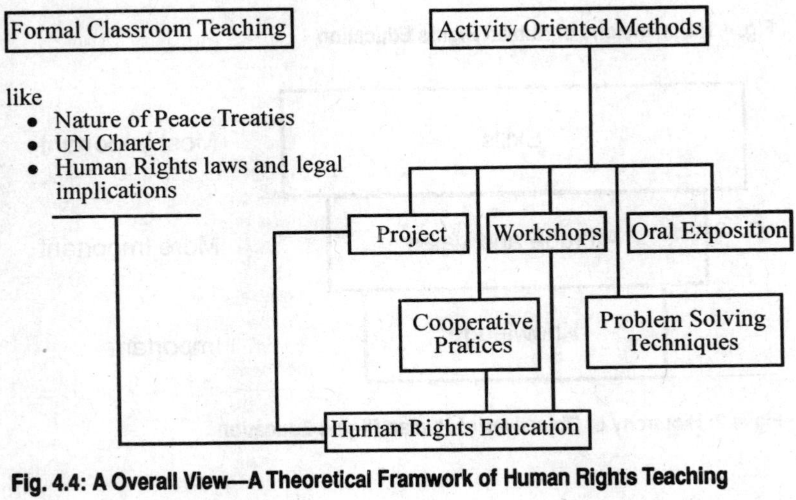

Fig. 4.4: A Overall View—A Theoretical Framwork of Human Rights Teaching

AIMS AND OBJECTIVES OF HUMAN RIGHTS AND EDUCATION

Education for Human Rights should aim at imparting knowledge, inculcating right attitudes and values and developing the skills of the students.

A. Knowledge	Concepts	(i) Historical development (ii) Infringements/violations of Human Rights in one's own and other countries (iii) Concept and scope of Human Rights (iv) Problems of under-developed/ developed countries on Human Rights, their obligations and responsibilities
	Understanding of development process	(i) Understanding of the environment and Human rights over a period of time (ii) International understanding and the cultural heritage of humanity (iii) The United Nations System (iv) Universality of Human Rights
B. Attitudes and Values	Attitudes	Attitude formation is more important than knowledge acquisition. It includes: (i) Self-respect (ii) Respect of others (iii) Commitment to peace and justice
	Values	Procedural values are considered to be more important than social attitudes. These include: (i) Fairness and respect for truth (ii) Tolerance, freedom and open mindless
C. Skills	Intellectual skills	Problem solving, critical thinking and communicative competence
	Action skills	To be able to participate and communicate in human rights concerns

Knowledge

(1) *Historical Background.* Students should know the major "sign posts" in the development of human rights. Significant examples in history of the denial of rights should be studied (e.g., political domination, slavery persecution of the Jews, etc.)

(2) *Infringements of Human Rights within one's Own Country.* Students should appreciate that no country has a clean reputation. The observance of human rights is a matter of degree. Some ways in which violations of human rights are monitored, for example by the Indian National Commission for Human Rights, should be dealt with.

(3) *Violations of Human Rights in Other Countries.* Students should be made aware of all kinds of inequalities and injustices including the results of gender bias and racism.

(4) *Knowing about Other People and Groups.* Students should develop the ability to approach people of different backgrounds confidently and without arrogance.

(5) *Equality of People.* Students should develop an understanding of the principles of democracy and equality which underli a belief in the equality of all peoples, and the right of all people to life, freedom and self-determination.

(6) *Maintenance of Peace.* Students should develop an understanding of the nature of negative and positive peace, of different types of war and their causes and effects, of the importance of cultural, economic and political relation between countries, and, of the importance of international law and collective security in maintaining peace.

(7) *Understanding of Rights.* Students should develop an understanding of their rights or responsibilities as citizens of local, national and global communities and of the need to eliminate discrimination and other threats to human rights from various sources.

(8) *Development.* Students should develop an understanding of the need for balance between economic growth and social development in the interests of the sustainable development and the overcoming of poverty and social justice. They should learn about forms, approaches and stages of development and causes of poverty.

(9) *Environment.* Students should be familiarised with the significance of ecological balance, effects of environmental degradation and destruction, and the need to balance economic growth and conservation through a process of sustainable development.

(10) *Understanding of the International Cultural Heritage.* Students should develop an understanding of cultural diversities as well as universality of human culture which give quality to life and contribute to world cooperation and peace.

(11) *The United System.* Students should develop an understanding of the roles of the United Nations, its efforts to protect human rights and to solve international problems.

(12) *Universality of Human Rights.* Students should understand the concept of universality of human rights.

Attitudes and Values

More importance should be given to attitude formation than knowledge acquisition.

(1) *Respect.* In order to give due respect to other students, students should develop respect for themselves. Students should have respect for others especially for those with cultural, family and national backgrounds different from their own.

(2) *Ecological Concern.* Students should have respect also for the natural environment and the overall place which they hold in the web of life. Also, they should have a sense of responsibility for both the local and global environment.

(3) *Commitment to Peace and Justice.* Students should value genuinely democratic and peaceful principles and processes and should be ready to work for a more just and peaceful world at interpersonal, local, national, regional and international levels.

(4) *Open-mindedness.* Students should be willing to approach different sources of information, people and events with a critical and open mind.

(5) *Empathy.* Students should be able to imagine sensitively the viewpoints and feelings of other people, particularly those belonging to groups, cultures and nations other than their own.

(6) *Solidarity.* Students should develop a genuine interest in and commitment to common concerns and the search for solutions to problems, beginning at the local level.

(7) *Toleration*. Students should be aware of their own prejudices and develop attitudes of toleration, mutual understanding and respect among all social groups.

Skills

(1) *Critical Thinking*. Students should be able to approach issues with an open and critical mind and be willing to change their opinions in the face of new evidence and rational argument. They should be able to recognise and challenge bias, indoctrination and propaganda.

(2) *Multi-disciplinary*. Students should be able to use a multi-disciplinary approach to solving problems.

(3) *Cooperation*. Students should be able to appreciate the value of cooperating on shared tasks and be able to work cooperatively with other individuals and groups in order to achieve a common goal.

(4) *Imagination*. Students should be able to develop images of what a better world might look like, not only in their own communities but also in other communities and in the world as a whole.

(5) *Assertiveness*. Students should be able to communicate clearly and assertively with others, avoiding aggression, which denies the rights of others, and avoiding passivity which denies their own rights.

(6) *Controversial Thinking*. Students should study controversial issues using a critical analysis of all points of view and avoiding dogma and values relativism. In evaluating alternative viewpoints and evidence, they should exercise and develop thinking skills and clarify their own values and opinions.

(7) *Conflict Solution*. Students should be able to analyse different conflicts in an objective and systematic way and be able to suggest a range of solutions to them. Where appropriate, they should be able to implement solutions themselves.

(8) *Tolerance for Ambiguity*. Students should develop a capacity to realise that not all problems can be immediately solved while simultaneously being optimistic about their eventual solution.

(9) *Participation*. Students should be developing an ability to influence and participate in decision-making within their local community, and also at national, regional and international levels.

(10) *Communicative Competence*. Students should be able to communicate in at least one language other than their own to facilitate their contact with people of other countries and their understanding of other cultures.

CURRICULUM OF HUMAN RIGHTS EDUCATION

Curriculum should include the following elements:

1. Main Concepts Associated with Human Rights – Different Human Rights
2. Manifestations and Phenomena
3. Dimensions of Human Rights – Discrimination, Violence, etc.
4. Perspectives and Levels of Human Rights – Individual Rights
5. Role of UNO and Its Agencies in the Promotion of Human Rights
6. Mechanism for checking violation of human rights
7. National Human Rights Commission
8. Rights of Deprived Sections and Their Safeguards
9. Constitutional Provisions Relating to Human Rights.

1. Inclusion of Main Concepts Associated with Human Rights

Rights

1. Children's Rights
2. Civic Rights (and sometimes Civil Rights, Civil Liberties)
3. Cultural Rights
4. Economic Rights
5. Human Rights
6. Legal Rights
7. Minority Rights
8. Natural Rights
9. Political Rights (often linked as Civil and Political Rights)
10. Social Rights (often linked as Economic and Social Rights).
11. Welfare Rights
12. Women's Rights

2. Manifestations and Phenomena

1. Discrimination
2. Conflict
3. Environmental protection
4. Equality (and equality of treatment)
5. Fairness
6. Freedom (freedom to and freedom from)
7. Genocide
8. Injustice
9. Justice
10. Oppression
11. Peace
12. Self-determination
13. Toleration
14. Welfare
15. Violence (and Structural Violence).

3. Dimensions of Human Rights

	Life		*Liberty*		*Security*
		From		*To*	
		Political-Legal		Economic - Social - Cultural	
		Slavery, exile, arbitrary, arrest, retroactive laws, punishment	Speech, assembly, participation in government, fair trial	Work, just remuneration, reasonable standard of living, social security	
Individual	Preser-vation of life	Discrimination according to race, religion, sex	Nationality, religion, marriage, movement, privacy, property	Life of dignity, rest and leisure, free education for development of personality, enjoyment of cultural life	Against torture and degrad-ing treat-ment
Group/ country	Against genocide	Discrimination	Existence self-determi-nation		

4. Perspectives and Levels of Human Rights

1	**Individual rights**	• Rights are possessed by individuals • Rights are opposed to the state • Rights are enforced through individuals' claims against the state • Rights are observed through the absence of interference by individuals and institutions.
2	**Social and collective rights**	• Rights are held by groups or classes • Rights are defined and activated through the state • Rights are enforced through administrative action • Rights are achieved through actions by institutions and the state.
3	**European rights**	• Continuous development of rules for communal life which reflect and encourage a gradual convergence of national laws • The European Court of Human Rights • The European Convention on Human Rights • The Case Law of the European Commission.
4	**International rights**	Human Rights violations as a result of the political and economic relationship between the First and the Third World and the Western and Eastern hemisphere.
5	**Global rights**	• Idea of an indivisible world • Consciousness of the "interlocking-crises" • Idea of the unity of humankind • Rights must be extended to all human beings and all human groups and peoples.

Source: P. Weinbrenner, Prof., University of Bialefeld, Germany.

MAIN ENTRIES ON CURRICULUM IN THE '*ENCYCLOPAEDIA OF HUMAN RIGHTS*' (1989)

Abortion
Affirmative Action
Aggression
Amnesty Laws
Apartheid
Armed Conflict
Assembly and Association
Bonded Labour
Centre for Human Rights
Chemical Weapons
Conscientious Objection to Military Service
Constitutional Councils
Council of Europe
Death Threats

Debt Bondage
Derogation
Domestic Violence
Drug Abuse
Education
Environment
Equality
Food
Forced Labour
Foreign Dept.
Freedom of Information
General Assembly
Genocide
Health
Holy See
Homelessness
Hostages
Illiteracy
International Bill of Rights
International Court of Justice
International Labour Organisation
Judiciary
League of Nations
Legal Aid
Mentally Ill Persons
Migrant Workers
Nationality
OAS
OAU
Permanent Court of Arbitration
Persons Born out of Wedlock
Political Rights
Poverty
Privacy
Property
Public Emergency
Refugees
Remedy
Right to Development
Right to Leave any Country, including One's Own, and to Return to One's Own Country
Right to Life
Right to Organise
Science and Technology
Self-Determination
Shelter
Social Security
Standard of Living
State of Emergency
Thought, Conscience and Religion
Torture
Transsexualism
UNESCO
UNICEF
UN-Charter
UN – Development Fund for Women
UN – Environment Programme
UN – High Commissioner for Refugees
UN – Institute for Training and Research
UN- University
Universal Declaration of Human Rights
World Food Council
World Health Organisation
World Intellectual Property Right.

HUMAN RIGHTS EDUCATION AS THE CORE OF THE SCHOOL CURRICULUM

Human rights as the core of the school curriculum is illustrated in Fig. 4.5

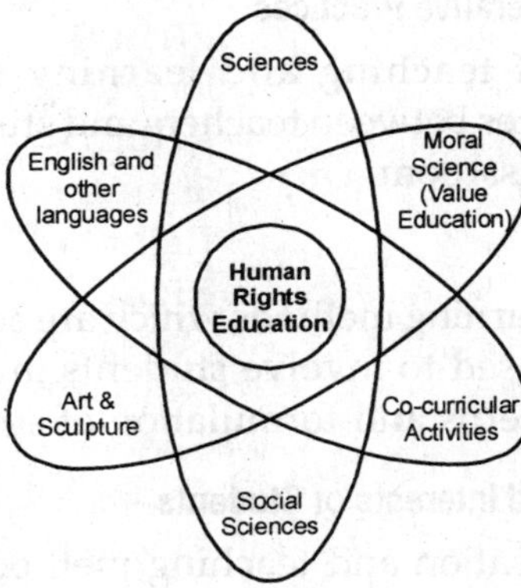

Fig. 4.5: Human Rights Education as the Core of the School Curriculum

TEXTBOOKS ON HUMAN RIGHTS RESEARCH

Major contents of the textbooks should cover are illustrated in Fig. 4.6

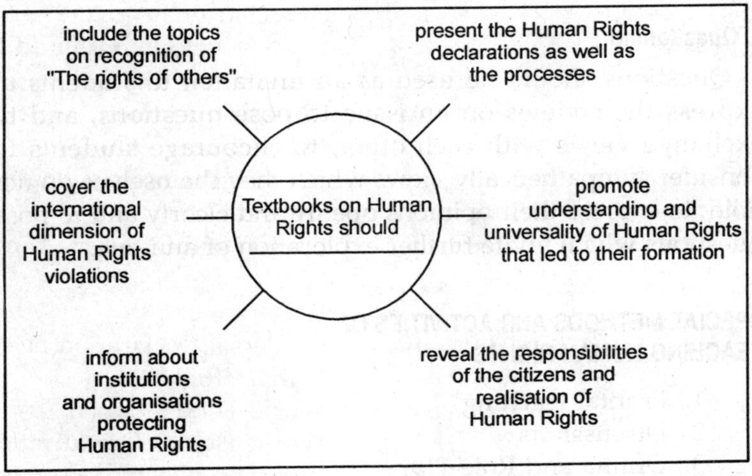

Fig. 4.6: Textbooks on Human Rights

GENERAL METHODS AND ACTIVITIES OF TEACHING HUMAN RIGHTS

Important methods of teaching human rights are:

1. Promotion of Cooperative Practices

The process of teaching and learning should promote cooperative practices between teachers and students and among students in the classroom.

2. Active Methods

Teaching and learning methods which are active and process-based should be used to involve students in the investigation of issues and concerns and formulation of solution.

3. Learning Needs and Interests of Students

Content organisation and teaching methods to be matched to different learning needs and interests of students of different ages and abilities.

4. Oral Exposition

The students to be helped to acquire and develop a language for discussion of human rights issues and to master the concepts associated with Human Rights.

5. Questioning

Questions should be used as an invitation to students to express their views on an issue to pose questions, and to exchange views with each other, to encourage students to consider sympathetically views which they themselves do not hold, to express their opinions openly and clearly and to pose questions which invite further exploration of an issue.

SPECIAL METHODS AND ACTIVITIES OF TEACHING HUMAN RIGHTS

1. Frontal teaching
2. Discussions
3. Drama and Role-Play

4. Practical activities—organisation of adult education centres, community service etc.
5. Projects
6. Workshops
7. Visits to orphanages, old age homes
8. Organising human rights days
9. Collecting documents on human rights
10. Displaying human rights materials on bulletin boards
11. Organising debates.

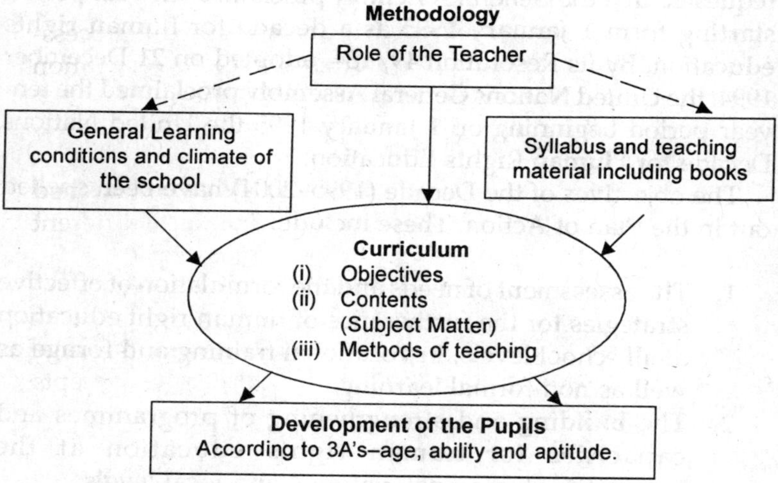

Fig. 4.7: Contents and Methodology of Teaching Human Rights

OBSTACLES TO HUMAN RIGHTS EDUCATION

Ignorance of historical processes which shape and change one's awareness of human rights.

Incompetence as far as the citizens' chances of and the responsibilities for the protection of human rights are concerned.

Indifference arising from such incompetence and the feeling of powerfulness.

Imbalance in the perception of human rights violations and implementation.

Instrumentalisation of human rights as a means of legitimising power interests.

Intolerance through fear, the lack of self-esteem and improper and inadequate readiness.

UNITED NATIONS DECADE FOR HUMAN RIGHTS EDUCATION (1995–2004)

By Resolution 1994/51, the Commission on Human Rights requested that the General Assembly proclaim a ten-year period starting form 1 January 1995 as a decade for human rights education. By its Resolution 49/184, adopted on 21 December 1994, the United Nations General Assembly proclaimed the ten-year period beginning on 1 January 1995 the United Nations Decade for Human Rights Education.

The objectives of the Decade (1995–2004) have been spelled out in the Plan of Action. These include:

1. The assessment of needs and the formulation of effective strategies for the furtherance of human right education at all school levels, in vocational training and formal as well as non-formal learning.
2. The building and strengthening of programmes and capacities for human rights education at the international, regional, national and local levels.
3. The coordinated development of human rights education materials.
4. The strengthening of the role and capacity of the mass media in the furtherance of human rights education.
5. The global dissemination of the Universal Declaration of Human Rights in the maximum possible number of languages and in other forms appropriate for various levels of literacy and for the disabled.

The General Assembly appealed to all governments 'to contribute to the implementation of the Plan of Action and to step up their efforts to eradicate illiteracy and to direct education towards the full development of the human personality and to the strengthening of respect for human rights and fundamental freedoms' and urged governmental and non-governmental educational agencies to intensify their efforts to establish and implement programmes of human rights education, in particular by preparing and implementing national plans in this field.

The United Nations High Commissioner for Human Rights was requested to coordinate the implementation of the Plan of Action. The Centre for Human Rights of the Secretariat (In 1997, the Centre was merged with the Office of the High Commissioner for Human Rights), and the Commission on Human Rights in cooperation with Member States, human treaty-monitoring bodies, other appropriate bodies and competent non-governmental organisations, were asked to support his efforts. Specialised Agencies and United Nations programmes were invited to contribute, within their respective spheres of competence, to the implementation of the Plan of Action.

The General Assembly called upon international, regional and national non-governmental organisations, in particular those concerned with women, labour, development and the environment, as well as all other social justice groups, human rights advocates, educators, religious organisations and the media, to increase their involvement in formal and non-formal education in human rights.

SUGGESTIONS FOR STRENGTHENING PROGRAMMES FOR HUMAN RIGHTS EDUCATION

The United Nations High Commissioner for Human Rights, in its mid-term global evaluation of the progress made towards the achievements of the objectives of the United Nations Decade for Human Rights Education (1995-2004), submitted to the UN Secretary General made recommendations under the following heads:

I. Overall Recommendations. These cover: (1) Human Rights Education: Concepts and Methods. (2) Content of Human Rights Education. (3) Programmes on Human Rights Education. (4) Evaluation, Research and Monitoring. (5) Mass Media and Freedom Information. (6) Resources.

II. National Level Recommendations.

III. Regional Level Recommendations.

IV. International Level Recommendations.

I. Overall Recommendations

Set out below are overall recommendations directed at all principal actors and for implementation at all levels.

Human Rights Education: Concepts and Methods

(1) Value-oriented human rights education alone is insufficient. Human rights education should make reference to human rights instruments and mechanisms of protection, and to procedures for ensuring accountability.

(2) Creative participatory teaching methods that are relevant to peoples' lives should be used, and human rights should be introduced as a holistic framework.

(3) Gender sensitivity should be emphasised in all educational activities.

(4) An enabling environment for human rights educators (including the provision of information, training, facilities, equipment and protection from harassment) should be ensured.

(5) Priority should be given to sustainable approaches (i.e., training of trainers, integration of human rights into all relevant training and education curricula etc.).

Content of Human Rights Education

Activities for human rights education should address the following issues:

(1) Economic, social and cultural rights;

(2) Good governance;

(3) Impunity, and international criminal tribunals to deal with crimes against humanity;

(4) Human rights defenders (and the related United Nations declaration), racism and discrimination.
(5) The link between development and human rights should be stressed.
(6) The universality and indivisibility of human rights should be emphasised.

Programmes on Human Rights Education

(1) Sufficient attention should be paid to ensure that the human rights education needs of children and young people, as well as of adults, are met.
(2) Interaction among children and youth belonging to different ethnic communities should be promoted. Human rights education should be fostered within and outside school curricula.
(3) Human rights education should be promoted in all educational initiatives aimed at adults.
(4) Human rights education efforts aimed at the following targets should be increased:
   (a) local government officials, community leaders (both secular and religious);
   (b) legal and paralegal service providers;
   (c) rural populations and illiterate people;
   (d) women and girls;
   (e) vulnerable groups, such as people with HIV/AIDS, people with disabilities, minorities and the elderly;
   (f) non-state actors, such as multinational corporations, trade and financial organisations (World Trade Organisation, World Bank, International Monetary Fund etc.).

The utilisation of the United Nations Decade for Human Rights Education for mobilisation and the establishment of partnerships should be increased.

Evaluation, Research and Monitoring

Evaluation and studies and research of long-term impact should be undertaken in order to better understand which approaches work best and why, and in order to elaborate evaluation criteria. Every project on human rights education should incorporate the development of indicators to evaluate qualitative impact.

Mass Media and Freedom of Information

(1) Mass media strategies that would effectively promote human rights should be developed. Such strategies might include the following elements:
   (a) Media focus on human rights monitoring;
   (b) Increasing the use of the media by non-governmental organisations;
   (c) Training of media professionals on mechanisms for human rights protection;
   (d) Involvement of the community of artists;
   (e) Use by the media, when appropriate, of techniques of social marketing.

(2) Law reform policies and practices that improve access to information and strengthen mechanisms that facilitate the flow of information and freedom of the press and other media should be promoted and implemented more vigorously. Human rights education should focus on such law reform policies and practices.

(3) The possibilities offered by new information technologies in furthering human rights education should be better exploited, and access to such technologies should be increased. Existing programmes supporting the online development of projects on human rights education should be strengthened and new programmes implemented.

Resources

(1) Good practices for human rights education should be identified, compiled and disseminated.

(2) Organisational capacity-building in human rights education should be fostered.

(3) Funding for human rights education should be increased.

(4) Research on issues related to human rights education should be enhanced in academic institutions and human rights institutes.

(5) When appropriate, alliances with the business sector should be developed in support of human rights education.

II. National Level

(1) Governments should reaffirm the commitments and obligations that they have already made in respect of human rights education and accelerate their pace of implementation so as to realise significant achievements by the end of the Decade.

(2) Governments should promote the development of national strategies for human rights education which are comprehensive (in terms of outreach), participatory (in terms of involvement of all relevant actors), effective (in terms of educational methodologies) and sustainable (over the long-term). Such strategies could be embodied in a national plan of action for human rights education.

(3) Human rights education should be included as a component of national development plans and of other relevant national plans of action (general plans of action on human rights or those relating to women, children, minorities, indigenous peoples etc.).

(4) All governmental and non-governmental actors recognise, in a spirit of mutual respect, each other's potential and capacities in furthering human rights education. Partnerships should be established where cooperation (rather than co-option) is furthered. Maximum use should be made of existing programmes, materials and resources.

(5) Systems for better coordination of effort and greater cooperation among the various governmental agencies should be developed.

(6) Non-governmental organisations should develop and implement strategies to encourage Governments to fulfil their obligations to integrate human rights education into all forms and levels of education for children, youth and adults, and should monitor those strategies.

(7) International resources and materials should be adapted to local linguistic and cultural contexts.

III. Regional Level

(1) Key regional human rights education organisations, institutions, agencies and networks should be supported (or, if necessary, established) to develop further the human rights education capacity within regions, including support for regional meetings, training of trainers, online networking, sharing of region-specific materials etc.

(2) Region-specific programmes or coordination systems to maximise the participation of national entities (whether governmental or non-governmental) in programmes on human rights education should be developed. Such region-specific programmes can be linked to existing regional programmes supported by the United Nations.

(3) Strategies should be developed for the wider distribution of materials on human rights education through regional networks.

(4) Links should be established with regional mass media, social development and other groups to encourage the inclusion of human rights in their training programmes.

(5) Existing regional intergovernmental organisations should be encouraged to integrate human rights education into their programmes and to allocate additional resources in that regard within the framework of the Decade.

(6) Work with regional, education-related intergovernmental organisations should be enhanced in order to promote human rights education.

IV. International Level

(1) United Nations institutions should adopt a system-wide approach to the Decade. An effective coordination system should be developed and the role of the Office of the High Commissioner for Human Rights in such a system should be strengthened.

(2) Effective human rights training should be undertaken for all United Nations staff.

(3) Human rights education should be included in the agenda of the special session of the General Assembly on the follow-up to the World Summit for Children, 2001.

(4) The Office of the High Commissioner, as requested by the General Assembly, should monitor the developments in human rights education that take place during the Decade. In this regard, Governments should provide adequate means to enable the Office to fulfil that role.

(5) UNESCO, through its network of national commissions, should play an active part in encouraging Governments to develop human rights curricula for formal education and to take steps to ensure that school environments are conducive to human rights education.

(6) United Nations treaty bodies should emphasise the obligations of States parties with regard to human rights education by actively seeking detailed information during their review of the reports of State parties. Inadequacies in addressing priority target audiences should consistently be identified by treaty bodies as an area of concern. In addition, treaty bodies should perform a clearing-house role by sharing with Governments approaches and strategies that have proven successful elsewhere, and should keep the Office of the High Commissioner informed of major national developments in human rights education.

(7) The capacity for human rights education of national presences of intergovernmental organisations (United Nations resident coordinators, field presences of the Office of the High Commissioner for Human Rights, United Nations information centres, national and local offices of United Nations agencies etc.) should be strengthened so that they can provide technical support to national and local activities for human rights education.

(8) Intergovernmental organisations should facilitate collaboration between governmental institutions and non-governmental organisations at the national level.

(9) Educational materials developed by international organisations should be made easily accessible, distributed free of charge and translated into local languages.

(10) The potential support and contribution to human rights education by non-state actors, including the business community, as well as development, trade and financial organisations, should be explored.

Conclusions

(1) The right to human rights education has been reaffirmed in several international and regional human rights instruments. Adequate resources should be allocated by the responsible parties for the realisation of the right to human rights education.

(2) Human rights education is also an important strategy for achieving several important ends, notably empowerment, participation, transparency, accountability, the prevention of conflict, conflict resolution, peace-making and peace-building, and the more effective protection and realisation of all human rights for all.

5

Enforcement of Human Rights

CONCERN AND NECESSITY FOR ENFORCEMENT OF HUMAN RIGHTS

It is usually accepted that the sustainable achievement of the three agreed global priorities of peace, development and democracy cannot be achievement without enforcing human rights.

Enforcement of human rights can assure the rights of political choice and association, of opinion and expression, and of culture, the freedom from fear and from all forms of discrimination and prejudice, freedom from want and the right to employment and well-being.

Billions continue to live in poverty. There is huge disparity between the rich and the poor. There have been violent conflicts, increasingly ethnic in nature. Communities have been uprooted on account of violation of human nature.

Millions have been forced to leave their place of residence.

Political extremism and terrorism have targetted countless civilians. Unemployment, discrimination and social exclusion bedevil all societies.

HISTORICAL BACKGROUND FOR VIOLATION OF HUMAN RIGHTS

1. Worst forms of imperialism dominated most of the world in the past.
2. Landlordism compelled the tillers of the soil to lead the lives of serfs.
3. The factory owners and the capitalists have exploited the workers.
4. The Nazis persecuted lakhs of Jews.
5. Crores of people had to lead miserable lives in concentration camps during Communist regime in the erstwhile USSR.

6. South Africa practised 'apartheid.'
7. In several African countries there have been crimes of genocide.
8. Bonded labour still exists in several countries.
9. Drug abuse has been assuming alarming propositions.
10. Women have been suffering on account of gender bias.
11. Children have been abused.

To sum up, enforcement of human rights is needed for the dignity and development of not only of individuals but also of the nations. The objectives contained in the Preamble to the UN Charter – objectives of social progress, better standard of life etc., can only be achieved by enforcing human rights.

UN AND ENFORCING HUMAN RIGHTS

International Bill of Rights

Following are the mechanisms of enforcing human rights:

1. International Bill of Human Rights
2. Principal Human Rights Treaties
3. Expansion of Human Rights Law
4. Investigating Human Rights Violations and Protecting Human Rights
5. Preventing Human Rights through Technical Staff
6. Reforming National Laws
7. Conventional Mechanisms
8. United Nations Agencies Having Special Implementation Procedures

Over the years, the UN has adopted several covenants declaration and instruments which are legally binding on the members and they are obliged to respect the procedures for their implementation.

The Covenants elaborate the rights identified in the Universal Declaration of Human Rights.

The Covenants form part of the Bill of Human Rights.

The United Nations strives to create a culture of human rights around the world.

The broadest legally binding human rights agreements

negotiated under UN auspices are the International Covenant on Civil and Political Rights and the International Covenant on Economic, Social and Cultural Rights.

Both were adopted in 1966 and entered into force in 1976. They take the Universal Declaration a step further by making provisions legally binding. A majority of the world's countries are parties to the two Conventions, thereby opening the door to international monitoring of their human rights practices.

Along with the Universal Declaration, they comprise the International Bill of Rights.

Consensus was reached in 1966, and the United Nations General Assembly adopted the *International Covenant on Economic, Social and Cultural Rights* and the *International Covenant on Civil and Political Rights* that year. The preambles and articles 1, 2, 3 and 5 are virtually identical in both International Covenants. Both Preambles recognise that human rights derive from the inherent dignity of human beings. Article 1 of each Covenant affirms that all peoples have the right of self-determination and that by virtue of that right they are free to determine their political status and to pursue their economic, social and cultural development. Article 2, in both cases, reaffirms the principle of non-discrimination, echoing the Universal Declaration, while Article 3 stresses that States should ensure the equal right of men and women to the enjoyment of all human rights. Article 5 of both Covenants echoes the final provision of the Universal Declaration, providing safeguards against the destruction or undue limitation of any human right or fundamental freedom. Two *Optional Protocols* elaborate certain provisions of the Covenant on Civil and Political Rights, one providing for complaints by individuals, the other advocating the abolition of the death penalty.

When they entered into force in 1976, the two International Covenants made many of the provisions of the Universal Declaration effectively binding for States that ratified them. These two International Covenants, together with the Universal Declaration and the Optional Protocols, comprise the International Bill of Human Rights.

THE UNITED NATIONS HUMAN RIGHTS MACHINERY

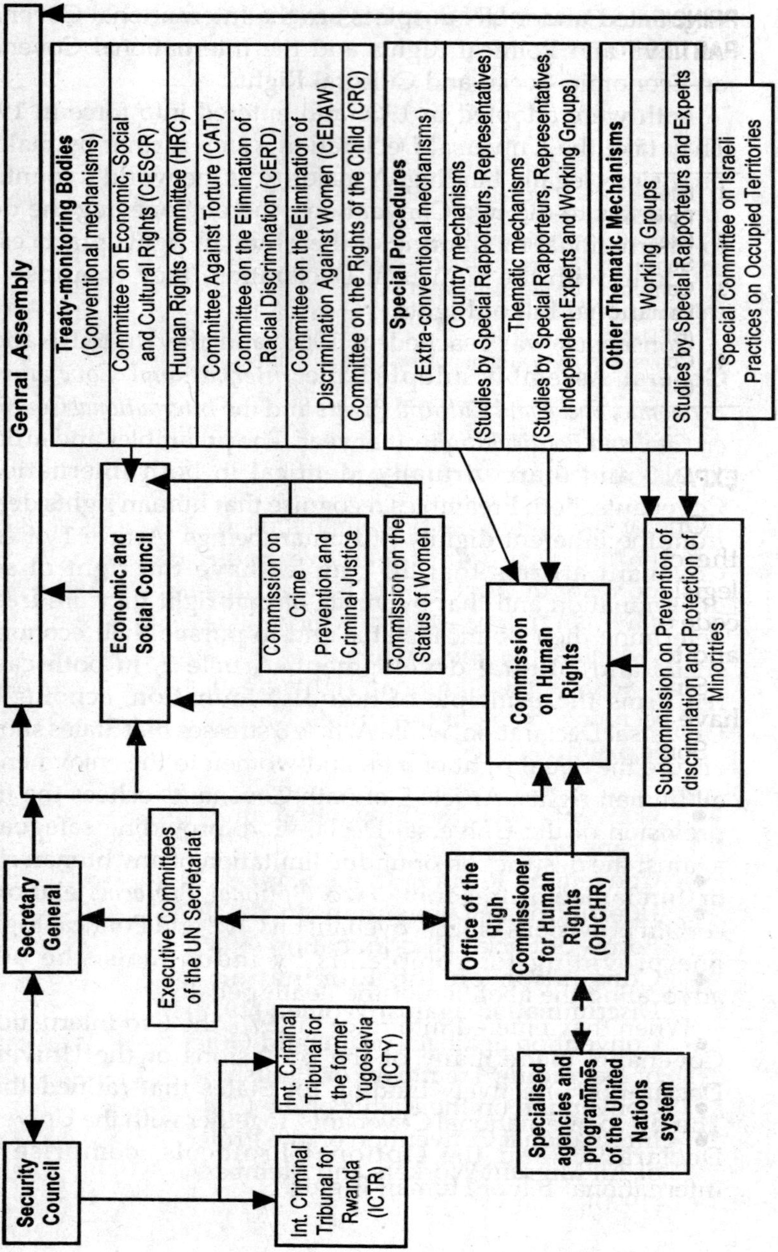

PRINCIPAL HUMAN RIGHTS TREATIES AND THE NUMBER OF STATE PARTIES TO THEM

	Treaty	*Year of Adoption*	*Entry into Force*	*Number of States Parties*
1.	International Covenant on Civil and Political Rights (ICCPR)	1966	1976	151
2.	International Covenant on Economic, Social and Cultural Rights (ICESCR)	1966	1976	148
3.	Convention on the Elimination of All Forms of Discrimination against Women (CEDAW)	1979	1981	174
4.	Convention on the Rights of the Child (CRC)	1989	1990	192

EXPANSION OF HUMAN RIGHTS LAW

One of the greatest achievements of the United Nations is the creation of a comprehensive body of human rights legislation. For the first time in history, there exists a universal code of human rights — one to which all nations can subscribe and to which all people can aspire.

Since 1948, some 80 human rights treaties and declarations have been negotiated at the United Nations.

Some examples are:

- Convention on the Prevention and Punishment of the Crime of Genocide (1948)
- Convention Relating to the Status of Refugees (1961)
- International Convention on the Elimination of All Forms of Racial Discrimination (1965)
- Convention on the Elimination of All Forms of Discrimination against Women (1979)
- Convention against Torture and Other Cruel, Inhuman or Degrading Treatment or Punishment (1984)
- Convention on the Rights of the Child (1989)
- International Convention on the Protection of the Rights of All Migrant Workers and Members of Their Families (1990)

As observed by Kofi Annan, United Nations Secretary General, "Ever since its inception, the United Nations has worked to refine and define international jurisprudence affecting human rights. Human rights are now a permanent feature of United Nations work for peace and a crucial factor in international relations."

INVESTIGATING HUMAN RIGHTS ABUSES AND PROTECTING HUMAN RIGHTS

Over the years, the United Nations has developed different methods to investigate human rights abuses and to press for remedial action.

Experts known as special rapporteurs or representatives gather facts, visit prisons, interview victims, and make recommendations on how to increase respect for human rights.

They investigate situations in specific countries and conduct thematic studies on such issues as torture, religious intolerance, racism, the sale of children and violence against women.

Each year they send thousands of urgent cables to Governments requesting the release of prisoners, the commutation of death sentences or other vital action.

Working groups have been established to investigate such issues as involuntary disappearances and arbitrary detention.

Their reports highlighting human rights violations help to mobilise international attention.

PREVENTING ABUSES HUMAN RIGHTS THROUGH TECHNICAL ASSISTANCE

Human rights agreements depend on the cooperation of Governments and people. The United Nations offers technical assistance to Governments in the following areas to promote human rights:

Reforming National Laws

Supporting democratisation and advising on electoral procedures.

Assisting in the drafting of national laws and preparation of national reports.

Strengthening national and regional institutions, such as courts and school systems.

Training criminal justice personnel – judges, lawyers, prosecutors and police.

UNITED NATIONS HUMAN RIGHTS MONITORING MECHANISMS

At the heart of the United Nations monitoring system are the two types of human rights monitoring mechanisms. The so-called conventional mechanisms refer to the specific committees formally established through the principal international human rights treaties. These "treaty bodies" monitor the implementation of the individual conventions by the States parties.

Over the years, the United Nations has also developed an independent and ad-hoc system of fact-finding outside the treaty framework, which is referred to as extra-conventional mechanisms or "special procedures." Independent experts report in their personal capacity as special rapporteurs or as members of working groups.

Treaty Bodies (Conventional Mechanisms)

Treaty bodies have been set up for the six core United Nations human rights treaties to monitor States parties' efforts to implement the provisions of the international instruments.

1. The *Committee on the Elimination of Racial Discrimination* (CERD) monitors the implementation of the International Convention on the Elimination of All Forms of Racial Discrimination. Composed of 18 independent experts, the Committee began its work when the Convention entered into force in 1969 and is the oldest treaty body.
2. The *Human Rights Committee* (HRC) monitors the implementation of the International Covenant on Civil and Political Rights. Composed of 18 independent

experts of recognised competence in the field of human rights, the Committee was established when the Covenant entered into force in 1976. The First Optional Protocol, which entered into force together with the Covenant, authorises the Committee to consider also allegations from individuals concerning violations of their civil and political rights. The Committee is also concerned with the Second Optional Protocol on the Abolition of the Death Penalty.

3. The *Committee on the Elimination of Discrimination Against Women* (CEDAW), composed of 23 independent experts, has monitored the Convention on the Elimination of All Forms of Discrimination against Women since 1981.
4. The *Committee on Economic, Social and Cultural Rights* (CESCR) monitors the International Covenant on Economic, Social and Cultural Rights. Composed of 18 internationally recognised independent experts in the relevant fields, the Committee was established by the Economic and Social Council in 1985, nine years after the Covenant entered into force. Unlike the other committees, whose members are elected by the States parties to the respective convention and report to the General Assembly, the members of the Committee on Economic, Social and Cultural Rights are elected by ECOSOC, to which they report.
5. The *Committee Against Torture* (CAT) monitors the Convention against Torture and Other Cruel, Inhuman or Degrading Treatment or Punishment. Composed of 10 independent experts, the Committee was established in 1987.
6. The *Committee on the Rights of the Child* (CRC), composed of 10 independent experts, has monitored the Convention on the Rights of the Child since 1991.

The Committees may call upon Governments to respond to allegations and may adopt decisions and publish them along with criticisms or recommendations.

CONVENTIONS RELATING TO RACIAL DISCRIMINATION, TORTURE, WOMEN AND CHILDREN

Over 80 human rights treaties elaborate fundamental rights and freedoms contained in the International Bill of Human Rights, addressing concerns such as slavery, genocide, humanitarian law, the administration of justice, social development, religious tolerance, cultural cooperation, discrimination, violence against women, and the status of refugees and minorities. The following four Conventions, relating to racial discrimination, torture, women and children, are considered core human rights treaties, together with the two International Covenants:

- The *International Convention on the Elimination of All Forms of Racial Discrimination* (adopted in 1965/entry into force 1969) was a ground-breaking treaty defining and condemning racial discrimination. Calling for national measures towards the advancement of specific racial or ethnic groups, the Convention also makes the dissemination of ideas based on racial superiority or inspiring racial hatred punishable by law.
- The *Convention on the Elimination of All Forms of Discrimination against Women* (1979/1981) specifies measures for the advancement and empowerment of women in private and public life, particularly in the areas of education, employment, health, marriage and the family.
- The *Convention against Torture and Other Cruel, Inhuman or Degrading Treatment or Punishment* (1984/1987) bans torture and rape as weapons of war. In 1998, in a major effort to help torture victims and to step up international attempts to end torture, the United Nations declared 26 June as the annual International Day in Support of Victims of Torture.
- The *Convention on the Rights of the Child* (1989/1990) is the most universally ratified human rights Convention. Only two Member States, the United States and Somalia, are not yet parties to the Convention, which protects

children, among other things, from economic and sexual exploitation.

19.11 UNITED NATIONS AGENCIES HAVING SPECIAL IMPLEMENTATION PROCEDURES FOR THE PROTECTION OF HUMAN RIGHTS WITHIN THEIR OWN FIELDS OF COMPETENCE

There are two United Nations Specialised Agencies within which such procedures have been established: the United Nations Educational, Scientific and Cultural Organisation (UNESCO) and the International Labour Organisation (ILO).

1. UNESCO and Its Procedure

UNESCO's competence extends to the rights relating to education, science (including social science), and culture and communications, which includes freedom of opinion and expression, and freedom of the press.

The procedures whereby UNESCO can take action regarding the promotion and implementation of human rights are partly provided for by the conventions and recommendations it has adopted. The method used is a reporting and complaints system.

The UNESCO Convention against Discrimination in Education entered into force in (1962). By now more than eighty States have become parties to it. This Convention commits States Parties to a national policy which will promote equality of opportunity and treatment in matters of education. States Parties undertake to ensure, by legislation if required, that there is no discrimination in the admission of pupils to educational institutions, nor any discrimination in the treatment of students. Foreign nationals are assured of the same access to education. The measures for implementation are based on a system of reports from the participating States which are examined by a special Committee on Convention and Recommendations. The reports and comments of the Committee are then submitted to the General Conference of UNESCO. The only further action taken is in the form of resolutions passed by the General Conference on the basis of the issues raised.

Good Office Commission

To supplement and strengthen this system, a Conciliation and Good Office Commission was created under a protocol to the Convention to deal with complaints from States alleging that another State Party is not giving effect to the provisions of the Convention. The Commission's mandate is to seek an amicable solution or, failing this, to make a recommendation which could include a request to the International Court of Justice for an opinion (the latter procedure, however, has never been applied).

2. International Labour Organisation (ILO) and Promotion of Human Rights

The ILO, which has been in existence since 1919 and became a United Nations Specialised Agency in 1946, seeks to achieve social justice through its activities in the social and labour fields. The basis of ILO action for human rights is the establishment of international labour standards and the supervision of the implementation of these standards by Member States of the organisation.

The ILO is a tripartite organisation, which means that all policy-making bodies of the organisation are composed of representatives of governments, employers and workers, who participate on an equal footing in the decision-making and procedures of the organisation.

International labour standards are adopted by the main body of the ILO, the International Labour Conference, in form of conventions or recommendations. The conventions, when ratified by States, are binding upon them. The conventions relate to the basic human rights concerns of the ILO, such as freedom of association, abolition of forced labour, freedom from discrimination in employment and occupation, child labour, etc. They also lay down standards in such fields as conditions of work, occupational safety and health, social security, industrial relations, employment policy and vocational guidance, and provide for the protection of special groups, such as women, migrants and indigenous and tribal

INTERNATIONAL HUMAN RIGHTS INSTRUMENTS

There are over 80 international human rights instruments today, and some are listed below. The core human rights treaties, which have established treaty bodies to monitor their implementation, are marked with an asterisk. Also listed is the year of adoption of a treaty and, where applicable, the year it entered into force.

I. Charter of the United Nations (1945)

II. International Bill of Human Rights

(1) Universal Declaration of Human Rights (1948)
(2) International Covenant on Economic, Social and Cultural Rights (adopted 1966, entry into force 1976, 137 ratifications)*
(3) International Covenant on Civil and Political Rights (adopted 1966, entry into force 1976, 140 ratifications)*
(4) First Optional Protocol to the International Covenant on Civil and Political Rights, allowing individuals to submit complaints to the Human Rights Committee (adopted 1966, entry into force 1976, 92 ratifications)
(5) Second Optional Protocol to the International Covenant on Civil and Political Rights, aimed at the abolition of the death penalty (adopted 1989, entry into force 1991, 33 ratifications).

III. Prevention of Discrimination

(1) ILO Convention concerning Employment and Occupation Discrimination (1958, 1960)
(2) UNESCO Convention against Discrimination in Education (1960)
(3) Declaration on the Elimination of All Forms of Racial Discrimination (1963)
(4) International Convention on the Elimination of All Forms of Racial Discrimination (1965, 1969, 150)*
(5) International Convention on the Suppression and Punishment of the Crime of Apartheid (1973, 1976, 101)
(6) Declaration on the Elimination of All Forms of Intolerance and of Discrimination Based on Religion or Belief (1981)

(7) UNESCO Declaration on Race and Racial Prejudice (1978)
(8) Declaration on the Rights of Persons Belonging to National or Ethnic, Religious and Linguistic Minorities (1992).

IV. Human Rights of Women

(1) Convention on the Political Rights of Women (1952,1954,110)
(2) Declaration on the Elimination of All Forms of Discrimination against Women (1967)
(3) Declaration on the Protection of Women and Children in Emergency and Armed Conflict (1974)
(4) Convention on the Elimination of All Forms of Discrimination against Women (1979, 1981, 161)*
(5) Declaration on the Elimination of Violence against Women (1993).

V. Rights of the Child

(1) Declaration on the Rights of the Child (1959)
(2) Declaration on the Protection of Women and Children in Emergency and Armed Conflict (1974)
(3) Declaration on Social and Legal Principles relating to the Protection and Welfare of Children, with Special Reference to Foster Placement and Adoption Nationally and International (1986)
(4) Convention on the Rights of the Child (1989, 1990, 191)*.

VI. Human Rights in the Administration of Justice

(1) Declaration on the Protection of All Persons from Being Subjected to Torture and Other Cruel, Inhuman or Degrading Treatment or Punishment (1975)
(2) Convention against Torture and Other Cruel, Inhuman or Degrading Treatment or Punishment (1984, 1987,105)*
(3) Basic Principles on the Independence of the Judiciary (1985)
(4) Body of Principles for the Protection of All Persons under Any Form of Detention or Imprisonment (1988)

(5) Principles on the Effective Prevention and Investigation of Extra-legal, Arbitrary and Summary Executions (1989)
(6) Basic Principles for the Treatment of Prisoners (1990)
(7) Declaration on the Protection of All Persons from Enforced Disappearances (1992).

VII. Social Welfare, Progress and Development

(1) Declaration on Social Progress and Development (1969)
(2) Declaration on the Rights of Mentally Retarded Persons (1971)
(3) Universal Declaration on the Eradication of Hunger and Malnutrition (1974)
(4) Declaration on the Use of Scientific and Technological Progress in the Interests of Peace and for the Benefit of Mankind (1975)
(5) Declaration on the Rights of Disabled Persons (1975)
(6) Declaration on the Right of Peoples to Peace (1984)
(7) Declaration on the Right to Development (1986)
(8) International Convention on the Protection of the Rights of All Migrant Workers and Members of Their Families (1990).

VIII. Slavery, Servitude, Forced Labour and Similar Institutions and Practices

(1) Slavery Convention (1926, 1927, 40)
(2) Convention for the Suppression of the Traffic in Persons and of the Exploitation of the Prostitution of Others (1949, 1951, 72)
(3) Protocol amending the Slavery Convention (1953, 1953, 59)
(4) Supplementary Convention on the Abolition of Slavery, the Slave Trade, and Institutions and Practices Similar to Slavery (1956, 1957, 117).

IX. War Crimes and Crimes Against Humanity, Including Genocide

(1) Convention on the Prevention and Punishment of the Crime of Genocide (1948, 1951, 125)
(2) Convention on the Non-Applicability of Statutory

Limitations to War Crimes and Crimes against Humanity (1968, 1970, 43)

(3) Principles of International Cooperation in the Detection, Arrest, Extradition and Punishment of Persons Guilty of War Crimes and Crimes Against Humanity (1973).

X. Humanitarian Law

(1) Geneva Convention for the Amelioration of the Condition of the Wounded and Sick in Armed Forces in the Field (1949, 1950)

(2) Geneva Convention for the Amelioration of the Condition of Wounded, Sick and Shipwrecked Members of Armed Forces at Sea (1949, 1950)

(3) Geneva Convention relative to the Treatment of Prisoners of War (1949, 1950)

(4) Geneva Convention relative to the Protection of Civilian Persons in Time of War (1949, 1950)

(5) Protocol Additional to the Geneva Conventions of 12 August 1949, and relating to the Protection of Victims of International Armed Conflicts (Protocol I) (1977, 1979)

(6) Protocol Additional to the Geneva Conventions of 12 August 1949, and relating to the Protection of Victims of Non-International Armed Conflicts (Protocol II) (1977, 1978).

XI. Nationality, Statelessness, Asylum and Refugees

(1) Convention relating to the Status of Refugees (1951, 1954, 132)

(2) Convention relating to the Status of Stateless Persons (1954, 1960, 44)

(3) Convention on the Nationality of Married Women (1957, 1958, 66)

(4) Protocol relating to the Status of Refugees (1966, 1967, 132)

(5) Declaration on Territorial Asylum (1967)

(6) Declaration on the Human Rights of Individuals Who Are Not Nationals of the Country in Which They Live (1985).

XIII. Right to Self-determination

Declaration on the Granting of Independence to Colonial Countries and Peoples (1960).

XIII. Freedom of Association

(1) ILO Convention on Freedom of Association and Protection of the Right to Organise (1948, 1950)

(2) ILO Convention on the Right to Organise and Collective Bargaining (1949, 1951).

XIV. Employment

(1) ILO Convention concerning the Promotion of Collective Bargaining (1981, 1983)

(2) ILO Convention concerning Employment Promotion and Protection against Unemployment (1988, 1991)

(3) ILO Convention concerning Indigenous and Tribal Peoples in Independent Countries (1989, 1991).

XV. Marriage, Family and Youth

Convention on Consent to Marriage, Minimum Age for Marriage and Registration of Marriages (1962, 1964, 47)

XVI. Right to Enjoy Culture, International Cultural Development and Cooperation

Declaration of the Principles of International Cultural Cooperation (1966).

Sources:

1. Manual on Rights-Based Education, UNESCO, Thailand, 2004.
2. Human Rights Today, UNO, 1998.
3. Teaching Human Rights, German Commission in UNESCO, 1993.

6

Mechanism in Schools for the Protection of Human Rights: NGOs, Press and Media

THE BEST INTERESTS OF EACH CHILD

The key principle in the Convention on the Rights of the Child (1989) which asserts that education must be designed and implemented with the best interests of each child in mind, necessitates identifying and eliminating factors that impede the child's learning. These include:

1. Curriculum which is ill-conceived to the age of the child i.e., is not according to 3A's – Age, Ability and Aptitude of the student.
2. Methodology of instruction which does not promote learning to learn.
3. School organisation which is authoritarian and rigid.
4. School discipline which is based on 'do's'.
5. Discriminatory admission process.
6. Discriminatory treatment to the students by the teachers.
7. Textbooks which do not promote open-mindedness, include material which is not conducive to democratic values.
8. Neglect of 4A scheme of education i.e., (1) availability, (2) accessibility, (3) acceptability and (4) adaptability.
9. Defective language policy which does not protect the language right of the child.
10. Lack of equal opportunities for education.

LEGAL PROHIBITION OF CORPORAL PUNISHMENT IN THE WORLD

Methods of teaching that use the threat of physical punishment as motivation to conform have been found incompatible with the core objectives and purposes of education. For this reason, the process of outlawing corporal punishment started in earnest in the 1990s, leading to changes throughout the world. Box lists countries which have legally prohibited corporal punishment in school, demonstrating how rapid this process of change has been in all regions of the world.

National Legal Prohibitions of Corporal Punishment in School

Albania, Andorra, Armenia, Austria, Azerbaijan, Bahrain, Belarus, Belgium, Bosnia and Herzegovina, Bulgaria, Burkina Faso, Cameroon, China, Colombia, Congo, Costa Rica, Croatia, Cyprus, Czech Republic, Denmark, Dominican Republic, Egypt, El Salvador, Eritrea, Estonia, Ethiopia, Fiji, Finland, France, Georgia, Germany, Greece, Guinea-Bissau, Honduras, Hong Kong, Hungary, Iceland, India, Indonesia, Iran, Iraq, Ireland, Israel, Italy, Japan, Kazakhstan, Kenya, Latvia. Liechtenstein, Lithuania, Luxembourg, Macedonia, Malawi, Maldives, Malta, Mauritius, Moldova, Monaco, Mongolia, Namibia, Netherlands, New Zealand, Norway, Oman, Philippines, Poland, Portugal, Qatar, Republic of Korea, Russia, Samoa, San Marino, Serbia, Slovakia, Slovenia, South Africa, Spain, Sri Lanka, Suriname, Sweden, Switzerland, Taiwan, Thailand, Trinidad and Tobago, Turkey, Uganda, Ukraine, United Kingdom, Uzbekistan, Zambia, Zimbabwe.

PROTECTION OF RIGHTS OF THE TRIBAL STUDENTS

Children belonging to the tribal families should be provided facilities to read and write in their own language or in the language most commonly used by the group to which they belong.

Students' Council and Parent Teachers Committee for the Protection of Children's Rights

Every school should have a student council to manage some

of the activities of the school and also to look into cases of students indiscipline.

Constitution of Parent-Teachers Committee for the Protection of Children's Rights

The function of the Committee would be to look into all cases of violation of child's rights.

CORE HUMAN RIGHTS OBLIGATIONS IN EDUCATION: MECHANISM OF PROTECTION OF HUMAN RIGHTS

The school system must ensure the four elements:

Availability. Obligation to ensure compulsory and free education for all children in the country within a determined age range, up to at least the minimum age of employment.

Obligation to respect parental freedom to choose education for their children, observing the principle of the best interests of the child.

Accessibility. Obligation to eliminate exclusion from education based on the internationally prohibited grounds of discrimination (race, colour, sex, language, religion, opinion, origin, economic status, birth, social status, minority or indigenous status, disability).

Obligation to eliminate gender and racial discrimination by ensuring equal enjoyment of all human rights in practice, rather than only formally prohibiting discrimination.

Acceptability. Obligation to set minimum standards for education, including the medium of instruction, contents and methods of teaching, and to ensure their observance in all educational institutions.

Obligation to improve the quality of education by ensuring that the entire education system conforms to all human rights.

Adaptability. Obligation to design and implement education for children precluded from formal schooling (e.g., refuge-seeking or internally displaced children, children deprived of their liberty, or working children).

Obligation to adapt education to the best interests of each child, especially regarding children with disabilities, or minority and indigenous children.

Obligation to apply indivisibility of human rights as guidance so as to enhance all human rights through education, such as the right to marry and raise a family, or the right to freedom from forced and child labour.

Development of the Ability to Learn

The current trend of ranking learners, according to their performance in tests that measure easily quantifiable learning outcomes has, paradoxically, jeopardised the general commitment to learning. Thus, rights-based education provides a useful pointer to the core objective of education, namely development of the ability to learn and to continue learning throughout life.

Right to Learn in the Mother-Tongue

The Convention on the Rights of the child emphasises that the school must guarantee the right of the child to receive instruction in the mother-tongue during the first stage of education.

CREATION OF PROPER ENVIRONMENT IN SCHOOL FOR THE DEVELOPMENT OF KNOWLEDGE, ATTITUDES AND SKILLS ABOUT HUMAN RIGHTS

School is said to be an idealised epitome of the family. It, therefore, is expected to provide a congenial, loving and vibrant environment. It must be remembered that the school is a place where the destiny of a nation is moulded. It is not merely a place for study which prepares for a certificate or a degree. It is a place where future citizens are trained, who are well-acquainted with their rights, responsibilities and the relations between those two elements. The school should 'therefore' ensure opportunities for self-discipline and social discipline. Its function is not only to provide for the teaching and practices of human rights but also to look after the human right of the students. As observed by S. Balakrishna Joshi, "A well-conducted school is a happy home, a sacred shrine, a social centre, a state in miniature — all beautifully blended into a synthetic structure."

The rights-based education demands that all upsets of child's personality should be suitable developed.

Summing Up

It may be stressed that the primary purpose of human rights education is to prevent abuses of powers. The school authorities should be fully alive to this.

NATIONAL HUMAN RIGHTS COMMISSION (NHRC)

A. Functions of the NHRC

In accordance with the provisions of the protection of Human Rights Act, 1993, National Human Rights Commission was constituted in India in 1994 and its functioning is regulated under the National Human Rights Commission (Procedure) Regulations, 1944. The Commission performs the following functions:

(a) inquire, *suo motu* or on a petition presented to it by a victim or any person on his behalf, into complaint of –
   (i) violation of human rights or abetment thereof; or
   (ii) negligence in the prevention of such violation, by a public servant;

(b) intervene in any proceeding involving any allegation of violation of human rights pending before a court with the approval of such court;

(c) visit, under intimation to the State Government, any jail or any other institution under the control of the State Government, where Demons are detained or lodged for purposes of treatment, reformation or protection to study the living conditions of the inmates and make recommendations thereon;

(d) review the safeguards provided by or under the Constitution or any law for the time being in force for the protection of human rights and recommend measures for their effective implementation;

(e) review the factors, including acts of terrorism, that inhibit the enjoyment of human rights and recommend appropriate remedial measures;

(f) study treaties and other international instruments on human rights and make recommendations for their effective implementation;

(g) undertake and promote research in the field of human rights;

(h) spread human rights literacy among various sections of society and promote awareness of the safeguards available for the protection of these rights through publications, the media, seminars and other available means;

(i) encourage the efforts of non-governmental organisations and institutions working in the field of human rights;

(j) such other functions as it may consider necessary for the promotion of human rights.

B. Composition of the National Human Rights Commission

1. A Chairperson who has been a Chief Justice of the Supreme Court.
2. One member who is, or has been, a judge of the Supreme Court.
3. One member who is, or has been, the Chief Justice of a High Court.

4,5. Two members to be appointed from amongst persons having knowledge of, or practical experience in matters relating to human rights.

6. The Chairperson of the National Commission for Minorities.
7. The Chairperson of the National Commission for Scheduled Castes and Scheduled Tribes.
8. Chairperson of the National Commission for Women.

C. Appointment of Chairperson and Other Members

The Committee to recommend the appointment of Chairperson and other members to the President, consists of

1. The Prime Minister —Chairperson
2. The Speaker of the House of the People —Member
3. Minister-in-charge of the Ministry of Home Affairs in the Government of India —Member

4. Leader of the Opposition in the House of the People — Member
5. Leader of the Opposition in the Council of States — Member
6. Deputy Chairperson of the Council of States — Member

D. Annual and Special Reports of the Commission

1. The Commission submits an annual report to the Central Government and to the State Government concerned and also special report, if any.
2. The reports along with the proposed action by the Government on the reports are laid before each House of Parliament or the State Legislature.

STATE HUMAN RIGHTS COMMISSION

Composition of the State Human Rights Commission

1. A chairperson who has been a Chief Justice of a High Court.
2. One Member who is, or has been, a Judge of the High Court.
3. One Member who is, or has been, a district Judge in that State.

4,5. Two Members to be appointed from amongst persons having knowledge of, or practical experience, in matters relating to human rights.

Appointment of Chairperson and Other Members of State Commission

1. The Chief Minister — Chairperson
2. Leader of the Opposition in the Assembly — Member
3. Minister-in-charge of the Department of Home in the State — Member
4. Leader of the Opposition in the Legislative Assembly — Member

HUMAN RIGHTS COURTS

The Protection of Human Rights Act, 1993 provides for the Constitution of Human Rights Courts by the States for providing speedy trials or offences arising out of violation of Human Rights.

NGO'S AND HUMAN RIGHTS

The United Nations has recognised the importance of a dynamic network of NGOs partnership worldwide for creating a pervasive culture of human rights.

NGOs and other representatives of civil society, such as academic institutions and citizens' groups, have been crucial to the United Nations Human Rights work since its inception – from the inclusion of human rights clauses in the Charter to the establishment of the Office of the High Commissioner for Human Rights. NGOs have also been key to developing human rights priorities in the major world conferences – particularly the agreements achieved on human rights in Vienna (1993), on population and development in Cairo (1994), on social development in Copenhagen (1995), on women's rights in Beijing (1995) and on food security in Rome (1996).

NGOs provide leadership in other areas, too. In the preparation of the Rome Conference, which approved the establishment of an International Criminal Court in July 1998, a well-informed and vocal NGO coalition was instrumental in pushing for a strong mandate for the Court. The coalition often led the debate on contentious issues such as the need for an independent prosecutor and the inclusion of the crime of aggression as one of the core crimes under the Court's jurisdiction. The strong NGO partnership with Governments and the United Nations ensured that the International Criminal Court, possesses the capacity to exercise its dual purpose of prosecuting individuals responsible for atrocities and deterring future barbarities.

The strength of non-governmental human rights organisations lies in their ability to mobilise public opinion, disseminate information and pressure Governments to conform to international human rights standards. There is great diversity among these NGOs. Some defend all human rights in general, while others protect the specific rights of particular vulnerable groups, such as women and children, or deal with urgent human rights issues, such as torture, enforced disappearances or the treatment of prisoners.

NGOs are vital actors in human rights advocacy: representing and protecting victims, providing expertise, collecting and disseminating information and encouraging human rights education. Among human rights NGOs, women's groups are among the most active in the world today, playing a vital role in the advancement and empowerment of women by increasing awareness of women's issues, as well as educating women in their human rights.

Among the most important international NGOs, mention may be made of the following:

1. Human Rights Watch
2. International Federation for Human Rights
3. Amnesty International.

In 1985, to protect human rights activists and NGOs, the Commission on Human Rights established a working group to draft a declaration aimed at guaranteeing individuals the right to publicly denounce violations, to form and participate in human rights NGOs and to communicate with international human rights organisations. In 1998, after more than 13 years of discussion, the Commission adopted the draft Declaration on the Right and Responsibility of Individuals, Groups and Organs of Society to Promote and Protect Universally, Recognised Human Rights and Fundamental Freedoms, also known as the Declaration on Human Rights Defenders. The Declaration is not a legally binding treaty, but clarifies and reinforces rights that are already recognised in existing international instruments.

PROTECTION OF HUMAN RIGHTS IN INDIA: THE PROTECTION OF HUMAN RIGHTS ACT, 1993 AND AS AMENDED IN 2000

The Protection of Human Rights Act, 1993 and as slightly amended in 2000 contains the following:

Chapter I

1. Short title, extent and commencement
2. Definitions.

Chapter II

The National Human Rights Commission

1. Constitution of the National Human Rights Commission
2. Appointment of Chairperson and other Members
3. Removal of a Member of the Commission
4. Terms and Conditions of Service of Members
5. Filling up Vacancies, etc.
6. Procedure to be followed by the Commission
7. Offices and other staff of the Commission.

Chapter III

Functions and Powers of the Commission

1. Functions of the Commission
2. Powers relating to inquiries
3. Investigation
4. Statement made by the persons to the Commission
5. Persons likely to be prejudicially affected to be heard.

Chapter IV

Procedure

1. Inquiry into complaints
2. Steps after inquiry
3. Procedure with respect to armed forces
4. Annual and special reports of the Commission.

Chapter V

State Human Rights Commissions
Constitution, Appointment and Functions etc.

Chapter VI

Human Rights Courts.

Chapter VII

Finance, Accounts and Audit.

Chapter VIII

Miscellaneous.

ROLE OF PRESS AND MEDIA IN HUMAN RIGHTS

Meaning and Significance of Press and Media

Nelson Henry has very rightly observed in *Media and Symbols*, "Educational institutions, left to themselves may not be successful in achieving the educational objectives of the developing societies without the support of the new media." New media, implying mass media, as channels of education gain relevance from their capacity to disseminate information to a great number of people (masses) and make the present educational programmes more effective and meaningful.

According to Dr. Marshall McLuhan whose books *The Gutenberg* and *Understanding Mass Media* throw a lot of light on the subject of mass media, it is the medium which is the message. This means that the medium by which a piece of information or knowledge is communicated to us exerts a profound influence on us. The effectiveness of a piece of information depends upon the medium through which it is imparted. Dr. McLuhan thinks that electronic media affect the sensibilities greatly because they tend to *massage* the senses. Thus the medium is not only the *message* but also the massage because it massages the sensory organs and stimulates them to respond actively. Therefore, it is important that the mass media be utilised in the classroom teaching so that the students may obtain sensory stimulation as a part of the process of instruction.

As observed by Wilbur Schramm in his book *Big Media-Little Media*, mass media can be made use of in education "as support models in two basic but overlapping ways."

1. They can be made part of environment into which learning activities are designed as seen in distance teaching institutions.
2. They can be brought into the environment as indirect partners or as tools in the hands of the teachers, by supplementing additional or supportive information that is educationally important and useful.

Mass media are means of impersonal communication via some medium, imported through mediated situation. Mass media are means or instruments of communication that reach large number of people or pupils with a common message. The matter may be printed like newspapers or it may take the form of radio, television and cinema. Carlton W.H. Erickson observes, "In recent years technology has swept through society from research laboratories into manufacturing communications, the space age, and finally now, into education."

In early times, the teacher was the only medium of communication for children. He taught his students orally. During the course of time the invention of the printing press, led to the printing of books. Then came newspapers. Now for quite sometime new mass media like radio and T.V. are increasingly used in education. They reach large members and also help in improving the quality of education.

Schools and colleges for long have been the sole medium for imparting information and aiding in the acquisition of knowledge. But with the technological development and fast expanding knowledge, new avenues of education have come up. These media disseminate information which the schools can no longer but needs to be integrated into the teaching-learning process.

The National Policy on Education 1986 and modified policy, 1992 has observed, "The media has profound influence on the minds of children. The mass media make the constraints of time and distance manageable. Modern educational technology must reach out to the most distant areas and the most deprived section of beneficiaries simultaneously with the areas of comparative affluence and ready availability."

Mass media serve some important functions. They are helpful

in teaching large number of people. They are helpful in the spread of human rights education. They are useful in making instruction more effective and meaningful.

The press and media highlight the need for the protection of human rights. They publish news regarding violation of human rights. They draw the attention of the government to various issues.

The press includes articles on the various dimensions of human rights. It creates awareness among different sections of population regarding their rights.

7

Quiz on Human Rights Education (With Answers)

1. What is the first human rights declaration adopted by the United Nations usually termed?
2. When was the Universal Declaration of Human Rights adopted?
3. Where was the Universal Declaration adopted?
4. Who were the key contributors to the drafting of the Universal Declaration of Human Rights?
5. How many articles does the Universal Declaration of Human Rights contain?
6. Can you name some of the rights championed by the Universal Declaration of Human Rights?
7. To whom does the Universal Declaration of Human Rights apply?
8. What is the slogan adopted for the Fiftieth Anniversary of the Universal Declaration of Human Rights?
9. When is Human Rights Day observed?
10. Why is Human Rights Day observed on 10 December each year?
11. When was the International Year for Human Rights?
12. Name some of the United Nations Commissions specialising in the field of human rights?
13. How many countries are members of the Commission on Human Rights?
14. Which United Nations Council selects the members of the Commission on Human Rights and on what basis?
15. Where does the United Nations Commission on Human Rights meet and for how long?
16. How many women have chaired the annual sessions

of the United Nations Commission on Human Rights since its first meeting in 1947? Who are they?

17. Which main committee of the General Assembly deals with most of the human rights issues?
18. Which United Nations declaration states that the objectives of economic activity should be the improvement of the social, economic, political and cultural well-being of individuals and not growth and profit?
19. Which office in the United Nations is responsible for dealing with human rights questions on a daily basis?
20. When was the Office of the High Commissioner for Human Rights established?
21. How many world conferences on human rights has the United Nations held? When and where were these conferences held?
22. Which important documents were adopted at the 1993 World Conference on Human Rights held in Vienna?
23. Where do human rights bodies usually hold their meetings?
24. What is the difference between a convention and a declaration?
25. Which human rights bodies can hear individual complaints of human rights violations?
26. How many human rights treaty bodies are there?
27. What are the six international human rights treaties monitored by the treaty bodies?
28. Which mechanisms have been devised by the United Nations to monitor human rights violations?
29. What are special rapporteurs and what do they do?
30. Can any victim of human rights abuses directly contact the Office of the High Commissioner for Human Rights?
31. Which United Nations human rights treaty has the highest number of country ratifications?
32. Which country originally suggested the idea of an international treaty on the rights of the child?
33. Which declaration was adopted by the United Nations in 1965 in order to protect the rights of young people?
34. When was the Convention on the Elimination of all

Forms of Discrimination against Women adopted by the General Assembly?

35. What United Nations convention deals with the rights of refugees?
36. The year 1995 was designated as the International Year for ________.
37. Which international declaration is aimed at religious intolerance?
38. When was apartheid eradicated in South Africa?
39. In which 10 places have United Nations human rights field offices been established.
40. What is the role of the human rights field offices?
41. Why is the Universal Declaration of Human Rights important to you?

ANSWERS

1. A Landmark Document entitled "The Universal Declaration of Human Rights."
2. December 10, 1948.
3. At the Palais de Chaillot in Paris (France).
4. (i) Eleanor Roosevelt (USA)
   (ii) Rene Cassin (France)
   (iii) Charles Malik (Lebanon)
   (iv) Peng Chun Chang (China)
   (v) Herman Santa Cruz (Chile)
   (vi) Alexandre Bogomolov/Alexei Pavlov (USSR)
   (vii) Lord Dukeston/Geoffrey Wilson (UK)
   (viii) William Hodgson (Australia)
   (ix) John Humphrey (Canada).
5. 30 Articles.
6. (i) Right to life, liberty and security of person.
   (ii) Right to education.
7. To each individual, regardless of gender, race, religion or cultural background.
8. Human Rights for All.
9. December 10 each year.
10. It commemorates the date of adoption of the Universal Declaration of Human Rights.
11. 1968.

12. (i) The Commission on Human Rights, (ii) The Commission on the Status of Women, (iii) Subcommission on the Prevention of Discrimination and Protection of Minorities.
13. 53 countries, representing all regions of the world.
14. The Economic and Social Council according to regional geographical distribution.
15. In Geneva for six weeks each year.
16. Three. (i) Eleanor Roosevelt (USA), (ii) Princess Ashraf Pahlavi (Iran), (iii) Purificacion Quisumbing (Philippines)
17. The Third Committee (Social, Humanitarian and Cultural)
18. The Declaration on the Right to Development, adopted by the United Nations General Assembly in 1986.
19. The Office of the High Commissioner for Human Rights in Geneva formerly known as the Centre for Human Rights.
20. 1993.
21. Two. One in Teheran (Iran), April 22—May 13, 1968 and the other in Vienna (Austria) - 14–25 June, 1993.
22. The Vienna Declaration and Programme of Action.
23. In Geneva.
24. A convention is a legally binding treaty coming into force upon ratification by a certain number of States. A Declaration is not legally binding but carries moral weight because it is adopted by the international community.
25. The Human Rights Committee that monitors the International Covenant on Civil and Political Rights, the Committee on the Elimination of Racial Discrimination and the Committee on Torture
26. Sixty-three bodies. Each Treaty Body monitors how countries implement a specific human rights treaty.
27. (i) Convenants on Civil and Political Rights.
    (ii) Economic, social and cultural rights.
    (iii) Conventions on the Rights of the Child.
    (iv) Elimination of All Forms of Discrimination against Women.
    (v) Elimination of All Forms of Racial Discrimination.

(vi) Elimination of All Forms against Torture.

28. (i) Conventional mechanisms (Treaty bodies to monitor compliance of State parties to conventions). (ii) Extra-conventional mechanisms (Special Rapporteurs, Working Groups and Special Representatives).
29. Special Rapporteurs are experts appointed by the Commission on Human Rights. They examine, monitor and publicly report on human rights situations and compliance of states with international instruments.
30. Yes.
31. The Convention on the Rights of the Child, adopted by the United Nations General Assembly in 1989.
32. Poland.
33. The Declaration on the Promotion among Youth of the Ideals of Peace, Mutual Respect and Understanding between People.
34. 1979.
35. The Convention Relating to the Status of Refugees, signed in Geneva in 1951.
36. Tolerance.
37. The Declaration on the Elimination of All Forms of Intolerance and of Discrimination Based on Religion or Belief, adopted by the General Assembly in 1981.
38. 1994.
39. (i) Abkhazia (Georgia), (ii) Brundu, (iii) Cambodia, (iv) Columbia, (v) Democratic Republic of the Congo, (vi) Gaza, (vii) Mongolia, (viii) Malawi, (ix) Rwanda, (x) Yugoslavia (former).
40. To assist in the development of national institutions for the Promotion and Protection of Human Rights and to conduct information campaigns on Human Rights among other victims.
41. It protects and promotes our individual rights.

Appendix 1

Human Rights Council

ESTABLISHMENT OF THE HUMAN RIGHTS COUNCIL

The Human Rights Commission set by the UN on June 21, 1946 was replaced by the Human Rights Council at its Sixtieth Session vide Resolution of March 15, 2006. The first meeting of the Council was held on June 19, 2006. It consists of 47 member States and is based in Geneva (Switzerland).

Chief Features of the Work of the Council

1. Promotion of human rights without distinction of any kind.
2. Promotion of human rights education.
3. Serving as a forum for dialogue on thematic issues on all human rights.
4. System of independent investigations of the violation of human rights by Member States of the UN.
5. Broad participation of the Civil Society in upholding the human rights.
6. Commitment of the Member States on human rights.
7. Elected members of the Council to be first in line for scrutiny relating to matters on human rights.
8. Suspension of members that commit gross and systematic violations of human rights.
9. Commitment of the members with the Council and its various mechanisms.

TEXT OF THE RESOLUTION (60/251) ADOPTED BY THE UN GENERAL ASSEMBLY ON THE ESTABLISHMENT OF THE HUMAN RIGHTS COUNCIL (15TH MARCH, 2007)

The General Assembly,

Reaffirming the purposes and principles contained in the

Charter of the United Nations, including developing friendly relations among nations based on respect for the principle of equal rights and self-determination of peoples and achieving international cooperation in solving international problems of an economic, social, cultural or humanitarian character and in promoting and encouraging respect for human rights and fundamental freedoms for all,

Reaffirming also the Universal Declaration of Human Rights and the Vienna Declaration and Programme of Action and recalling the International Covenant on Civil and Political Rights, the International Covenant on Economic, Social and Cultural Rights and other human rights instruments,

Reaffirming further that all human rights are universal, indivisible, interrelated, interdependent and mutually reinforcing, and that all human rights must be treated in a fair and equal manner, on the same footing and with the same emphasis,

Reaffirming that, while the significance of national and regional particularities and various historical, cultural and religious background must be borne in mind, all States, regardless of their political, economic and cultural systems, have the duty to promote and protect all human rights and fundamental freedoms,

Emphasizing the responsibilities of all States, in conformity with the Charter, to respect human rights and fundamental freedoms for all, without distinction of any kind as to race, colour, sex, language or religion, political or other opinion, national or social origin, property, birth or other status,

Acknowledging that peace and security, development and human rights are the pillars of the United Nations system and the foundations for collective security and well-being, and recognizing that development, peace and security and human rights are interlinked and mutually reinforcing,

Affirming the need for all States to continue international efforts to enhance dialogue and broaden understanding among civilizations, cultures and religions, and emphasizing that States, regional organizations, non-governmental organizations, religious bodies and the media have an important role to play in promoting tolerance, respect for and freedom of religion and belief,

Recognizing the work undertaken by the Commission on Human Rights and the need to preserve and build on its achievements and to redress its shortcomings,

Recognizing also the importance of ensuring universality, objectivity and non-selectivity in the consideration of human rights issues and the elimination of double standards and politicization,

Recognizing further that the promotion and protection of human rights should be based on the principles of cooperation and genuine dialogue and aimed at strengthening the capacity of Member States to comply with their human rights obligations for the benefit of all human beings,

Acknowledging that non-governmental organizations play an important role at the national, regional and international levels, in the promotion and protection of human rights,

Reaffirming the commitment to strengthen the United Nations human rights machinery, with the aim of ensuring effective enjoyment by all of all human rights, civil, political, economic, social and cultural rights, including the right to development, and to that end, the resolve to create a human Rights Council,

1. *Decides* to establish the Human Rights Council, based in Geneva, in replacement of the Commission on Human Rights, as a subsidiary organ of the General Assembly; the Assembly shall review the status of the Council within five years;
2. *Decides* that the Council shall be responsible for promoting universal respect for the protection of all human rights and fundamental freedoms for all, without distinction of any kind and in a fair and equal manner;
3. *Decides* also that the Council should address situations of violations of human rights, including gross and systematic violations, and make recommendations thereon. It should also promote the effective coordination and the mainstreaming of human rights within the United Nations system;

4. *Decides further* that the work of the Council shall be guided by the principles of universality, impartiality, objectivity and non-selectivity, constructive international dialogue and cooperation with a view to enhancing the promotion and protection of all human rights, civil, political, economic, social and cultural rights, including the right to the development;
5. *Decides* that the Council shall, inter alia:
   (a) Promote human rights education and learning as well as advisory services, technical assistance and capacity-building, to be provided in consultation with and with the consent of Member States concerned;
   (b) Serve as a forum for dialogue on thematic issues on all human rights;
   (c) Make recommendations to the General Assembly for the further development of international law in the field of human rights;
   (d) Promote the full implementation of human rights obligations undertaken by States and follow-up to the goals and commitments related to the promotion and protection of human rights emanating from United Nations conferences and summits;
   (e) Undertake a universal periodic review, based on objective and reliable information, of the fulfilment by each State of its human rights obligations and commitments in a manner which ensures universality of coverage and equal treatment with respect to all States; the review shall be a cooperative mechanism, based on an interactive dialogue, with the full involvement of the country concerned and with consideration given to its capacity-building needs; such a mechanism shall complement and not duplicate the work of treaty bodies; the Council shall develop the modalities and necessary time allocation for the universal periodic review mechanism within one year after

the holding of its first session;

(f) Contribute, through dialogue and cooperation, towards the prevention of human rights violations and respond promptly to human rights emergencies;

(g) Assume the role and responsibilities of the Commission on Human Rights relating to the work of the Office of the United Nations High Commissioner for Human Rights, as decided by the General Assembly in its resolution 48/141 of 20 December, 1998;

(h) Work in close cooperation in the field of human rights with Government, regional organizations, national human rights institutions and civil society;

(i) Make recommendations with regard to the promotion and protection of human rights;

(j) Submit an annual report to the General Assembly;

6. *Decides also* that the Council shall assume, review and, where necessary, improve and rationalize all mandates, mechanisms, functions and responsibilities of the Commission on Human Rights in order to maintain a system of special procedures, expert advice and a complaint procedure; the Council shall complete this review within one year after the holding of its first session;

7. *Decides further* that the Council shall consist of forty-seven Member States, which shall be elected directly and individually by secret ballot by the majority of the members of the General Assembly; the membership shall be based on equitable geographical distribution, and seats shall be distributed as follows among regional groups: Group of African States, thirteen; Group of Asian States, thirteen; Group of Eastern European States, six; Group of Latin American and Caribbean States, eight; and Group of Western European and other States, seven; the members of the Council shall serve for a period of three years and shall not be eligible for immediate re-election after two consecutive terms;

8. *Decides* that the membership in the Council shall be open to all States Members of the United Nations; when electing members of the Council, Member States shall take into account the contribution of candidates to the promotion and protection of human rights and their voluntary pledges and commitments made thereto; the General Assembly, by a two-thirds majority of the members present and voting, may suspend the rights of membership in the Council of a member of the Council that commits gross and systematic violations of human rights;
9. *Decides also* that members elected to the Council shall uphold the highest standards in the promotion and protection of human rights, shall fully cooperate with the Council and be reviewed under the universal periodic review mechanism during their term of membership;
10. *Decides further* that the Council shall meet regularly throughout the year and schedule no fewer than three sessions per year, including a main session, for a total duration of no less than ten weeks, and shall be able to hold special sessions, when needed, at the request of a member of the Council with the support of one third of the membership of the Council;
11. *Decides* that the Council shall apply the rules of procedure established for committees of the General Assembly, as applicable, unless subsequently otherwise decided by the Assembly or the Council, and also decides that the participation of and consultation with observers, including States that are not members of the Council, the specialized agencies, other intergovernmental organizations and national human rights institutions, as well as non-governmental organizations, shall be based on arrangements, including Economic and Social Council resolution 1996/31 of 25 July, 1996 and practices observed by the Commission on Human Rights, while ensuring the most effective contribution of these entities;

12. *Decides also* that the methods of work of the Council shall be transparent, fair and impartial and shall enable genuine dialogue, be results-oriented, allow for subsequent follow-up discussions to recommendations and their implementation and also allow for substantive interaction with special procedures and mechanisms;
13. *Recommends* that the Economic and Social Council request the Commission on Human Rights to conclude its work at its sixty-second session, and that it abolish the Commission on 16 June, 2006;
14. *Decides* to elect the new members of the Council; the terms of membership shall be staggered, and such decision shall be taken for the first election by the drawing of lots, taking into consideration equitable geographical distribution;
15. *Decides further* that the Council shall review its work and functioning five years after its establishment and report to the General Assembly.

72nd plenary meeting
15 March, 2006

Appendix 2

Recent UN Reports on Climate Change and Global Warming

INTRODUCTION

There is substantial evidence that human activities contribute to the build-up of 'Greenhouse gases' in the atmosphere, leading to a gradual rise in global temperatures. In particular, carbon dioxide is produced when fossil fuels are burned to generate energy, or when forests are cut down and burned. According to the Intergovernmental Panel on Climate Change, climate models predict that global temperatures will rise by about 1.4 and 5.8 degrees C (2.5-10.4 F) by 2100. This projected increase is larger than any climate change experienced over the past 10,000 years—with potentially significant impact on the global environment.

The United Nations Framework on Climate Change

To counter global warming, the 1992 *United Nations Framework Convention on Climate Change* was developed and signed in Rio de Janeiro. Under the Convention, developed countries agreed to reduce emissions of carbon dioxide and other greenhouse gases they release into the atmosphere to 1990 levels by 2000. These countries, which together account 60 per cent of annual carbon dioxide emissions, also agreed to transfer to developing countries technology and information to help them respond to the challenges of climate change. By May, 2004, 189 countries had ratified the Convention.

Report of the Intergovernmental Panel on Climate Change (1989) (IPCC)

United Nations negotiations on climate change are supported by the work of the **Intergovernmental Panel on Climate Change (IPCC)**, which was organized jointly in 1988 by UNEP and WMO. The Panel, a worldwide network of 2,500 leading scientists and experts, reviews scientific research on the issue.

In 1989, its finding that human activities could possibly cause changes in the global climate system led to negotiations on the climate change convention. By 2001, with access to new and more powerful computer models, the Panel found that there is "new and stronger evidence that most of the warming observed over the last 50 years is attributable to human activities".

IPCC Report 1995

The evidence presented by IPCC scientists in 1995 made it clear that the 1992 target, even if reached on time, would not prevent global warming and its associated problems. Additional reductions would be necessary. In 1997, countries that had ratified the Convention met in Kyoto, Japan, and agreed on a legally binding *Protocol* which developed countries are to reduce their collective emissions of six greenhouse gases by 5.2 per cent between 2008 and 2012, taking 1990 levels as the baseline. The Protocol also establishes several innovative "mechanisms" aimed at reducing the costs of curbing emission levels.

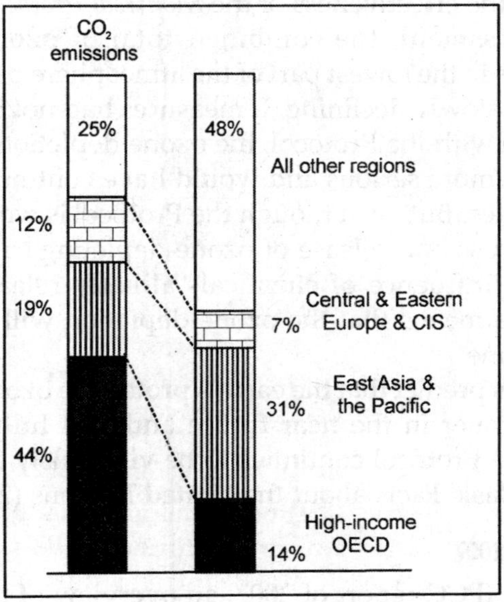

Fig. A-1.1: Carbon dioxide emissions originate disproportionaitley in high-income countries

Ozone Depletion: The ozone layer is a thin layer of gas in the upper atmosphere, about 12 to 45 kilometres above the ground, that shields the earth's surface from the sun's damaging ultraviolet rays. Exposure to increased ultraviolet radiation is known to result in skin cancer, and to cause unpredictable damage to plants, algae, the food chain and the global ecosystem.

UNEP helped to negotiate and now administers the historic *Vienna Convention for the Protection of the Ozone Layer* (1985), and the *Montreal Protocol* (1987) and its amendments. Under these agreements, developed countries have banned the production and sale of chlorofluorocarbons—chemicals that deplete the ozone layer. Developing countries must stop their production by 2010. Schedules are also in place to phase out other ozone-depleting substances.

Report of 2002

In 2002, a UNEP-WMO assessment of ozone depletion, prepared by more than 250 scientists from around the world, confirmed the effectiveness of the *Montreal Protocol*. According to the assessment, the combined total of ozone-depleting compounds in the lowest part of the atmosphere peaked in 1994 and is now slowly declining. If measures had not been taken in accordance with the Protocol, the ozone depletion would have been much more serious and would have continued for many more decades. But even though the Protocol is working well to reduce the use and release of ozone-depleting substances, the continuing influence of chemicals already released into the atmosphere means that the ozone depletion will continue for years to come.

Scientists predict that the earth's protective ozone shield will start to recover in the near future and will fully recover by 2050—if the Protocol continues to be vigorously enforced.

Source: Basic Facts about the United Nations (2004).

IPCC Report 2007

The first IPCC report of 2007, an overview of the science of global warming, said that it was 'very likely' or at least 90 per cent certain that mankind was to blame for most of the warming in the last half century.

The previous report in 2001 had put the probability at 'likely', or at least 66 per cent. The new report projected a 'best estimate' that temperatures would rise by 1.8 to 4.0 degrees Celsius this century.

The second report details the likely impacts of climate change around the global, such as on health, farming and water availability.

